PRINCETON, WV

On the
Skirmish Line

by
William Sanders

McClain Printing Company
P.O. Box 403
Parsons, WV 26287
1997

International Standard Book Number 0-9625273-6-x
Library of Congress Catalog Card Number 96-092641
Printed in the United States of America
Copyright © 1997 by William Sanders
Princeton, West Virginia 24740
All Rights Reserved

Prelude and Dedication

15 June 1994 –
Fifty-Year Anniversary
Return to Saipan Island

I had put World War II completely out of my mind. I had been happy to live my life in peace and opportunity. Life is always a series of skirmishes. With war, as with life in general, its how you come out in the end that matters. I never wanted to dwell on my war experiences in the Pacific against the Japanese. I had joined veteran's organizations and paid my dues, but I never attended a meeting. I did however, attend an annual reunion of the Marine's Second Division several times, just to see some of my friends who fought beside me. Otherwise, the war in the Pacific was just an interlude in my life's journey.

Then, I received an invitation to attend ceremonies for the Fiftieth Anniversary of the war on Saipan and Tinian Islands in World War II. My law office colleagues made it possible by paying my way. As a result Katherine and I spent five days on Saipan in the summer of 1994 – memories returned.

Fifty years ago we landed on the beach at Charan Kanoa, near the blasted hulk of the sugar mill. During the next several days we had advanced around Susupe Lake, Sugar Loaf Hill and Flame Tree Hill, and through the Japanese officers' park and homes in the outskirts of Garapan Town. At that time it seemed that Mount Tapotchau, the central island high point, was looking right down on us.

In our 1994 return to Saipan, we stayed at the plush Pacific Island Club. That hotel sits right on the very beach where, fifty years ago, our invasion force landed in the face of hostile fire.

It is a long taxi ride into Garapan town from Charan Kanoa, now renamed Chalan Kanoa. The distance between the town and the hotel is paved with a four-lane highway, lined with many stores, including a McDonald's restaurant. These days no one thinks of walking those four or five miles. Katherine and I got a cab from the hotel. When the meter hit seventeen dollars, and we were still a mile short of Garapan Town proper, I told the driver to let us out. Some natives saw us and hailed a police

Jeep. The police took us to the United States Memorial Park in north Garapan, still in the process of being built.

Katherine and I later hired a car and a driver who knew the island. We found the major places of my war involvement. We declined the side trip to Tinian, where I had spent eight days fighting through the jagged coastal coral rock jungle and saw little else of that island.

We found our former First Battalion campsite, with the grand eastern view of the airport and the sea. A natural bridge formation over a narrow road near the camp was gone, but the old cave still loomed on the cliffside above the site. Some elaborate mansion houses had since been erected in the area. One was owned by a very rich Italian/American, whom we dropped in on. It struck me that there were a lot of mixed breed chicken running all over this area. I'm sure they were descendants of my chickens of fifty years before.

Our driver James, the father of a nice young lady at the Dollar Rental Car Agency in the lobby of our hotel, was from Palau in the Caroline Island group. He had lived on Saipan for twenty years. He was a most helpful tour guide. We especially

Fifty-year anniversary parade on Coastal Boulevard by present-day Second Marine Division down from Okinawa.

enjoyed visiting James's friend, Don Flores. He had lived on Saipan Island all of his life. He was in charge of building a park

Katherine beside pillbox on our landing beach.

Golf course shoreline where my company killed 350 Japanese soldiers.

and shrine around the ruined Japanese fortifications at Magaciene Bay Beach.

These fortifications were massive and supplied by long cavernous tunnels. As on Tarawa, they could have resupplied men and munitions to oppose any landing there. We would have faced these fortifications had we landed in rubber boats as planned. While giving us a tour of the ruins, Don Flores cut open a fresh coconut with his machete, and offered us its milk to drink.

James also showed us what was once Tanapag Harbor, just north of Garapan. A typhoon had since obliterated the former harbor by filling in the ship channel. Nearby, James showed us an inland cove in a grove of trees where the Japanese high command had lived. James told us that here Amelia Earhart had been kept prisoner for a long time. Here she was executed as an American spy.

His account was based on the firsthand knowledge of an old native woman. This woman had been a house servant of the Japanese officers in that compound. Her account became common knowledge among the islanders before the woman died a few years ago. The account goes: Amelia Earhart was captured on Majura in the Palau, Caroline Islands group, and was brought to Saipan for detention and interrogation. Saipan was the Japanese main Pacific headquarters. Earhart was presumed to have knowledge of United States military plans and purposes. Earhart was probably as innocent and ignorant of any such plans as any other common United States citizen was at the time.

Knowing the irrational frame of mind of the Japanese from observing their suicidal behavior, I thoroughly believe this version. I well remember what a wholesome, down-to-earth person Amelia Earhart was when I interviewed her as editor of my high school newspaper. I am sure she could never convince her evil-minded captors of her sole motivation and purpose of proving to the world that women are as good as men as airplane pilots or in most any other field of endeavor. The day of women's servitude is fast ending. Amelia Earhart's spirit lives on.

We attended a big parade, through the town of Garapan, on the coastal road. We also attended banquets hosted by the Island Governor at the Hyatt Hotel grounds and near the central United States war memorial. All were attended by marines, navy and army personnel brought down from Okinawa and bases in Japan. Major General Harvey, Commanding General of today's

Second Division of Marines, was accompanied by his very impressive black Division Sergeant Major. The example of today's marines, navy and army personnel at these ceremonies was most impressive. We old veterans were a scraggly bunch by comparison, dressed in assorted tropical vacation attire.

Another banquet was held in the veterans' honor on the spacious deck of a modern LST (Landing Ship Tank), the USS San Bernadino. On the next evening, Japanese visitors, also there for their fifty-year reunion (at least the children and relatives of the veterans, since the veteran participants in the battle there were virtually wiped out) were entertained on the same ship.

Many descendents of the Japanese forces of fifty years ago were visiting the shrines, parks and hotels of the island. They came down from Japan in droves to shop and stay at the resort hotels and play golf. It's a several hour flight, compared with our two-day flight to attend this anniversary.

It was their fiftieth anniversary also. It made me think of our own American Civil War, fought mostly on our Southern soil. we southerners took a terrific beating and, as the losers, celebrate the war's memory more than the northerners. So it is on Saipan with the Japanese.

The island is now covered with shrines and memorial parks. Many honor the Americans who fought and died here, many more honoring the Japanese. While we were being feted and visiting these various memorials, an equal number of Japanese were circulating all over the place. These tourists were relatives of the vanquished defenders of the island. Their shrines and memorial at Suicide Cliff, Banzai Cliff and other places were well maintained and visited by both sides. This presented a very odd situation as we old veterans found ourselves milling and mixing with the children and relatives of the enemy we laid low fifty years before. It was just as well there was a language barrier and we couldn't discuss the events that transpired years ago.

The most spectacular Japanese park is at Marpi Point, on the north end of the island. Here our former enemy has designated a shrine. The "Last Command Post," was a huge cave the Japanese had converted to a fortified bunker. In it, a large room in the rear has a commanding outlook over a potential landing beach. Fifty years ago we had converted a small Japanese airfield on this end of the Island to serve our fighter planes.

At the picturesque sheer cliff overlooking the north point is another Japanese shrine and park. This one commemorates "Suicide Cliff." Here, the Japanese defenders had forced their wives and children off the cliff, then jumped themselves. Another cliff on the northeastern shore, with an even more elaborate park, commemorates "Banzai Cliff." Japanese soldiers without families had jumped to the rocky shoreline below. The floating dead bodies made ship navigation difficult.

At Mount Tapotchau, whose peak I had used as an observation post in my patrolling activities, the scene is now much different. The bare peak pillbox has been levelled off. In its place is a large white statue of "Christus," a native shrine to the "Prince of Peace."

Two U.S. Park Service researchers interviewed me on the landing beach by our hotel. They also took Katherine and me to the area of our intense nighttime fire fight. (see picture)

We found the scene of the fire fight located at the edge of a golf course belonging to the eleven-story high, 350 room, ($150 per night) Nikko Hotel. Built by the Japanese Airlines, this hotel is the largest of the several resort hotels now on the island. This is the favorite hotel for the multitude of Japanese visitors. At that very spot, our company lost twenty-seven men and lost all company officers except me. I am sure the builders and owners of this fabulous resort are unaware of the fact that their golf course is located at the site where 350 Japanese soldiers met their death at the hands of the "Able" Company Marines.

Amid all the modern improvements, its hard to recall that we slogged around that island and dug in every night. We dug foxholes with trenching tools and helmets as a matter of course, rather than expose ourselves to the night firing. We put out our rolls of barbed wire at night when we had time and when the concentration seemed thick out front, like on the Nikki hotel golf course.

At the Hyatt Hotel banquet, two young lawyers on the U.S. Attorney General's staff discovered I was an old lawyer. The next day they telephoned and invited Katherine and me to attend the monthly luncheon of the Marianas Islands Bar Association, as their guest speaker. We enjoyed learning of the nature of law and government in this U.S. Territory. I had a good feeling about the governance of the island as an American Territory. I was especially impressed by the good will shown to us by the islanders who were governing themselves under United States sponsorship.

It was wonderfully rewarding to see the obvious gratitude on the faces of Chamarro and Carolinian natives. The natives showed us pure welcome. They are now American citizens, entitled to social security, welfare and all of the perks of being U.S. citizens. I was relieved to find that the natives had not committed suicide. The suicides were exclusively Japanese, except for the few natives who had married Japanese.

We are now reconciled with the Japanese. They are our ally now. However, an old vet remembers. If the Japanese ever get back their army and navy, I fear it could all revert to pure pride and ambition, just as before. I prefer that we keep our Pacific policing power and military presence. Let the Japanese spend their money at island resorts.

I also discovered that the only casualty of my "Able" Company, whose body we were unable to recover, was later found on the jungle slopes of Tapotchau by a Platoon Sergeant Arthur Petty. Petty was on the Fifty-Year Anniversary Tour and, during our reminiscing, told of finding the skeleton and dog tags of Squad Leader Sergeant Stickles in an area we had searched for two days.

Upon returning home from the celebrations on Saipan, after parting with the other old veterans along the return route homeward, I decided to write this life story.

This is the story of the erratic course of Kind Providence in the life of a combat marine officer in World War II, followed by nearly fifty years of legal skirmishes in the courts of southern West Virginia and is told in collaboration with the writer's oldest son, David Hartley Sanders, now circuit judge in the Eastern Panhandle of West Virginia, as an exercise in reconciliation between father and son after the tumultuous Civil Rights and Vietnam years in our family and across the land.

The book is affectionately dedicated to my parents, my two deceased sisters, my wife Katherine and our four children.

On the Skirmish Line

Outline

Marriage and Military Government

Courthouses and Causes in Southern West Virginia

First Years at the Bar of Justice

Civil Rights -- Crossroads of Life and Practice

The Hand of Kind Providence Continued

Other Major Cases Remembered

Railway Cases

Practice Proliferates

Judges

Public Causes

Addenda

EARLY YEARS IN
COUNTY SEAT TOWN

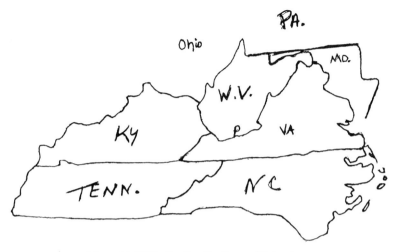

Map with "P" indicating the Town of Princeton.

I spent a carefree boyhood between World War I and World War II in my town of Princeton*, Mercer County, in southernmost West Virginia, a wonderful place to grow up. The town was a period piece.

Princeton's Early History

The town had been founded in 1837 on land owned by War of 1812 Captain William Smith. The site had been formerly owned by French Smith. William Smith was the high sheriff of Giles County, living adjacent to the area he set aside as Princeton, to serve as the county seat of new Mercer County, to be split off of Giles and the western portion of Tazewell County.

The town was laid off and mapped by CHA Walker, who spelled his first name on many deeds and instruments many ways, including Chrispianos and Chrispi Anos and was most

*Named after the Battle of Princeton, New Jersey and for George Washington's aide, General Hugh Mercer, killed there in the American Revolution.

familiarly known as Anos Walker.

Walker laid off the new town in an inverted "T" formation, with the top of the "T" as Main Street, east-west, and the stem of the "T", Walker Street, extending northward perpendicular from the center point of Main. At that junction of Walker and Main, a courthouse square was laid off.

In addition to the courthouse square, there were forty lots plus alleys and a public area reserved below the courthouse on Walker to preserve the bold "French Smith Spring" as town property and its first and only water supply.

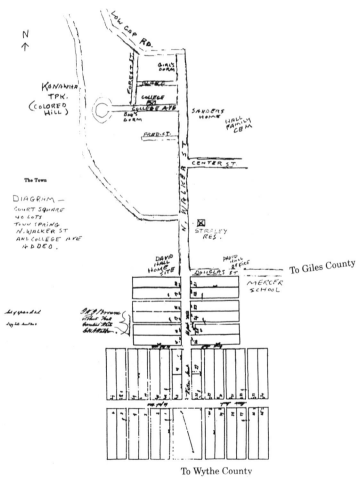

Main Street accommodated the courthouse, some stores and the first two churches, Baptist and Methodist. A Presbyterian church soon sprang up on Walker Street. Main Street was sixty feet wide, including sidewalks, which were first made of boards. Walker Street was sixty-six feet wide, including sidewalks, plus grass parkways on both sides of the street. Walker Street was extended northward after the Civil War through the twenty-acre homeplace of the county's first lawyer, David Hall, who sold his home to the Straley family for Confederate money in 1862 and moved to Indiana. The grass parkways continued in diminished width to my house at the top of the hill at the corner of College Avenue in the area that became known as College Hill. The parkways on Walker, in my lifetime, were reduced to accommodate larger and faster moving cars and trucks.

Thus, the town of forty lots, with courthouse square and spring, went through stages of growth. The city council entered an official Order on October 1, 1956, recognizing the abandonment of the Town Spring and quitclaiming any interest therein, in order to clear title for commercial development of the site. In my boyhood, the Town Spring was still in evidence.

Civil War

In the Civil War the original forty -lot town became a garrison of Confederate troops. In 1862, on orders from the garrison's commander, Colonel Jenifer, the town and courthouse were burned to deny foodstuffs and housing to the invading troops of General Jacob D. Cox's Ohio Army. Colonel Rutherford B. Hayes and his aide, Sgt. (later Lieutenant) William McKinley, set up headquarters on Walker Street in one of the few homes left standing after the fire. Many homes in the adjoining countryside had been burned by their Confederate owners. The Federals were thus unable to live off the land. They retreated to the Kanawha Valley.

The Federal advance on the railhead supply depot at Dublin, fifty miles further southeast, was delayed until 1864. When they advanced through Princeton again, skillful Union General George Crook lured the Confederate force away from town by feinting toward Lewisburg. Upon retaking Princeton, the Federals found that the Confederate Garrison had renamed the burned out area Fort Breckenridge, after a highly-respected Confederate General John C. Breckenridge, of Kentucky. This was in 1864. The Dublin railhead was finally destroyed and, thus, the war was shortened.

All of my life, my mother and other citizens with roots in the area used the term "numerous as Cox's Army."

Post War Controversy

The town gradually grew back following the Civil War, with rivalry from Athens, eight miles north and more central in the county, seeking to move the courthouse to their town. This contest waxed hot until the northern one-third of the county was cut off to form the new county of Summers and, thus, end the Athens' attempt – the burning of the town and courthouse had inspired this ambition of Athens to relocate the courthouse.

Coal, Railroads and Another Rivalry with a New Town

Coal mining began in the late 1800s, in the Pocahontas coal fields of western Mercer County and counties further west. Two rival railway lines came into the county to get the coal. The first, and most powerful, was the Norfolk & Western Railway. This railroad established a large rail yard as its eastern shipping point in a long valley on the Virginia border, a few miles from the town of Pocahontas, Virginia, where coal was first mined. The town of Bluefield grew up around this rail yard.

The older town of Princeton, which had been the natural center of the previously agrarian county, was more connected with eastern counties of Summers, Monroe and Giles. Princeton became the eastern shipping point of the smaller, but very profitable, Virginian Railway into the Wyoming County fields.

These two railroads ran on parallel lines, from the coalfields to the coast at Norfolk. To the east of Mercer County, in Greenbrier and newly-formed Summers County, the Chesapeake & Ohio Railroad built its line. It branched northward along the New River Gorge to Charleston, the state's capitol, to haul coal from the New River coalfields.

The powerful new Norfolk & Western coal mining and banking interests, centered in Bluefield, mounted an effort to have the county seat relocated to their new railway and coal shipping center. A second courthouse battle was waged. The initiative was defeated in a public vote when Princeton voted the numerous transient laborers then engaged in installing the Virginian Railway line and shops.

My Father Comes to Princeton to Practice Law

The Virginian Railway brought new life and growth to Princeton. My father arrived as the railway line was about to be built in 1906-1907. He came to Princeton on the advice of his University of Virginia Law School Dean Lile, in whose home he had lived at law school. My mother's family moved to Mercer County. They first came to the coal town of Bramwell from Floyd County, in Virginia's Blue Ridge Mountains, drawn by economic activity of the coal and railroads. My mother was born and raised in Bramwell before the family moved to Princeton.

My father became the city attorney and gained its city charter and incorporated the public water system. My father represented the Virginian Railway in a strike by its employees. Later still, in 1927, he successfully represented that railway before the Interstate Commerce Commission and resisted a takeover by the larger N&W. The takeover occurred many years later.

Born in 1917, I am a product of this railway town. I grew up in a neighborhood on a hillside bench along Walker Street. I was the second of three children born to Hartley and Ina Sanders. I had two sisters; Sarah, a couple of years older, and Caroline, a couple years younger.

I was told my name was to have been Daniel, after my great-great-grandfather on my father's side. However, my parents were building a home on Walker Street at the time of my birth and were renting a home from Daniel Carr, the town's principal builder. Mr. Carr lived next door to my parents' rented home on College Avenue. Mr. Carr had built many close-cropped brick homes in this neighborhood of College Avenue and Walker Streets.

My father built our new home opposite the campus of the Princeton Academy on Walker Street. This home, in which I

Walker Street from front lawn of courthouse, showing bank and lawyer's office building on right.

Bank and lawyer's office building from courthouse square lawn.

8

Top of Walker, with front of my home on left and looking toward the courthouse in the distance.

Corner of Walker and College, where the College Hill boys congregated.

9

would spend my childhood, was built by architect Wysong and contractor Caldwell. My father carefully drew up the construction contracts and performance bonds, etc. The house was constructed in the Greek Revival style of my father's beloved University of Virginia, as designed by Thomas Jefferson. With its white columns, it was built to resemble one of the Pavillions on the Lawn which are interspersed among the student rooms as classrooms and professors' homes of the original University Grounds.

Colored Hill and College Hill

College Avenue led off Walker Street and ended in Circle Drive. This neighborhood backed up to the part of town known as Colored Hill. Here the black residents of town lived. The freed colored had gradually settled along the old Kanawha Turnpike, the first road. This road had been used by invading forces in the Civil War. It connected with Walker Street.

Many blacks served as house and yard servants, walking back and forth from their homes to the homes of their white neighbors on Walker and College. The junction of Walker and College streets became known as College Hill. Colored Hill and College Hill comprised the northwest corner of the growing town. During my early childhood most of the town's streets were still unpaved. One reason "College Hill" may have seemed special was because the homes were readily accessible to colored help.

The Princeton Academy

College Hill got its name from the fact that the area had once been the property of the rapidly expanding Methodist Episcopal Church South (of the Holston Conference, including churches in east Tennessee, southwest Virginia and southern West Virginia.) Here, the church established the Princeton Academy in the early 1880s. The academy served as the first high school of the town and surrounding area.

A two-story stone school building had stood in the central hill area of present-day College Avenue. A wooden boys' dormitory was a short distance westward, toward Circle Drive, at the end of College Avenue. A two-story wooden girls' dormitory was located on Walker Street, a short distance north of the intersection of Walker Street and College Avenue. An open stone walled well was located beside Walker near the dormitory.

The school's last headmaster, the Reverend Eugene Blake, built an impressive brick home on Walker Street, next to the girls' dormitory. A street was laid just off Walker Street, paralleling College, named Blake Avenue. Blake Avenue remained unpaved and was, more or less, a wide alley, making a traffic pattern for the academy campus. The school closed around 1910, after about twenty-five years of existence.

The cut stone of the two-story classroom building was used by Mr. Carr to make foundations and basements for his many houses. At least one of the wooden dormitories burned down. They had both disappeared by the time I was born. The "college" campus and, thus, College Hill, was along Walker Street, the stem of the "T" formation of the original town.

FAMILY

Ina Sanders as college student.

Mother, Father, and Religion

Hartley placed Ina on a pedestal, adoring her and treating her like a queen. This did not mean, however, that he would forsake the Methodist faith of his father for the strong Baptist faith of his new wife.

My mother and my two sisters were staunch members of the First Baptist Church. My mother was principal soloist of the Baptist choir. Her sister, Vera, was the organist. Vera's husband, Tom Johnson, a car shop foreman at the Virginian Railway shops during the week, was the choir director. For many years, my mother was in great demand to sing solos at weddings and funerals.

My father and I were members of the Methodist Episcopal Church South, one block away from the Baptist church. Going to church on Sunday, sitting with my father in our accustomed pew, and singing the old hymns, was standard fare in my boyhood life. These hymns are indelibly recorded in my memory.

After church, our family would reassemble for Sunday dinner. The affairs and sermons of each church were discussed. Frequently, we visited each other's services at night or during the "revivals" which were annual events at both churches.

Life as a Boy

As a boy, I regularly played a game called "shinney." The rectangular foundation stones of what had been the academy's girls' dormitory formed our arena. The three Worrell boys had the duty of staking out the family cow in the grassy field next to the dormitory ruins. A series of holes were dug on four sides of the interior of the stone foundation. Each boy (no girls were allowed) had a pole or broomstick to guard his individual hole from being invaded by a tin can puck. As the other boys defended, the odd man would maneuver his puck around the court with his stick until getting the puck into one of the holes. The odd man would then put his foot over the hole displacing its owner, who then became the odd man out.

The game would go on and on in fast and furious fashion until the bruised shins of our young legs told us it was time to quit. Later, after upper Walker Street was paved, we played a slightly different version of the same hockey game on roller skates.

A less aggressive game played in the same old dormitory area was called "mumble peg." We played this game with our jack-knives. We would fully extend the long blade and only half extend the short blade. The object was to flip the knife with your finger as it stood on the short blade making the knife spin in the air. If it landed on the long blade, you scored higher points than if it landed on the small blade. The winner of the game won the privilege of driving a wooden matchstick in the ground with as many strokes of the knife as his score. The loser was required to root out the peg with his teeth. I don't recall the further details of this game. We played this during rest periods between the more vigorous games.

Most every boy owned a pocketknife as his prize possession, carried in his pants pocket, ready for whittling or fashioning a slingshot (more commonly referred to as our "gravel shooters"). Trading pocketknives among our peers was a regular practice as our first experience in the world of business.

The College Hill gang of boys kept busy with all sorts of self-conceived games. I don't know what the girls were doing, our world simply did not include them. If a rainy day cast a gloomy spell, we would assemble on the corner at Woolfolk's family porch, or at some out-of-the-way place, and play card games. We had backyard basketball courts with only one goalpost and our contests there went on in all sorts of weather. We had backyard football and touch football games. We had a vacant sandlot football field on Low Gap Road. This was our official field for playing the teams from across town. We had another, smaller, lot for practice on Frederick Court. We never knew who owned the vacant lots.

We assembled football, basketball and baseball teams in season with a ragged assortment of balls, uniforms, bats and gloves, largely derived from Christmas at the several homes. No families bought such items randomly through the years for this was the time of the Great Depression. The state of our ragged equipment did not diminish our enthusiasm.

Other sections of the town organized their own teams without any adult sponsorship whatever. Games were arranged by telephone. Park Avenue had its team, with Murray Stecker as captain. Straley Avenue had its teams, with Tim ("Emerson") Mann as captain. East Princeton had its team, with Ira ("Possum") Dishner, captain. I was the College Hill captain. A captain was the person who "got up" the team and contacted the other captains to set up the games.

It was all a very natural process, without any adult participation or even awareness. Our parents were busy enough with their own affairs. No one paid us any attention or attended our games. The teams were of all ages and sizes. When we skirmished in our own neighborhood backyards and along the Frederick Court path used by the colored people going to Colored Hill, we would choose up sides in the various games we contrived. I would usually choose one side by alternating selection with my good friend, George Woolfolk, who chose the other side. We wanted fairly evenly balanced teams so that the games would not be one sided and uninteresting.

I scarcely remember I mowed the lawn with a reel-type

17

mower with metal wheels, fed the dogs in their lot, fed the chickens and gathered the eggs and helped work the garden, fire the furnace and take out the ashes.

Halloween was the one night of the year we children were licensed to play tricks on uncaring neighbors. We left old people and the kid-loving folks alone. There was no such thing as trading "tricks for treats." This was a later invention designed to distract children from their time honored right to be heard and not seen.

There was a woman who had three kids that she wouldn't let come out and play like the rest of us. She would routinely chase all of us out of her yard for no reason at all. She would get it on Halloween. Diagonally across College Avenue lived an elderly couple whose oldest son had joined the Canadian forces before the United States became involved in World War I. He was the first hometown boy killed in that war. Their next son also joined the American forces in France. Those sons and three or four girls had grown and left the home, but the white-haired Mr. and Mrs. Kennedy kept a wonderful swing in good shape hanging from a very tall old oak tree in their backyard for all of the boys and girls who came along later. We never bothered these lovely people.

The woman with the three kids who made herself obnoxious at every turn received our attention on Halloween. She had called Pete McGlothlin, of our gang, an alley rat. That offended us all, as we were all alley rats. We travelled the alleys as often as we did the streets. The alley across the street from our home was a shortcut for Pete to his College Avenue home from school.

That alley was also a shortcut for all of us to an undeveloped, wooded, rocky area where we had a small sandlot football field on Frederick Court. There we gathered, about fifteen feet off the ground, in the crotch of a very ancient black oak tree. We called it "the knotty tree," since it had huge knots. These knots served as a ladder, and as seats in the crotch of the great tree where we congregated. The tree was also home to a lot of large, black ants, known in polite circles as carpenter ants.

Between the games, a good bit of marble playing took place. At the corner of College and North Walker streets, the ground between the sidewalk and the street had been worn bare of grass. We would mark a circle with a sharp stick or rock and each player put a certain number of marbles in the middle. We then took turns shooting the marbles out of the ring. As long as the shooter kept knocking one or more marbles out of the ring, he continued shooting. Only after a miss would the next man take his turn. We shot with "steelies," which were ball bearings out of old automobile wheels and/or agates, which were milk-colored, larger than standard-size marbles.

Some of the boys became amazingly expert as shooters and acquired the skill of the "drop shot." The steelie or agate was held between the thumb and the first finger. Propelled by the thumb from mid-air, this "missile" did not hit the ground until it struck the target, a marble, which it knocked out of the ring. The shooter would continue shooting from the place his steelie stopped. A few of the best shooters could just about clean the whole ring out in one turn, keeping all the marbles knocked out of the ring. I was forbidden to play marbles for keeps.

My knuckles got very dirty. Scrubbing all the dirt out, with a scrub brush in our home bathroom sink, was a major problem. It was a huge effort to get ready for church on Sunday or to look fairly civilized at school. The matter of dirt and grime on our bodies and clothes was the principal concern of our parents in our games. I remember the time when a bunch of us boys were feasting on Mr. Bert Calfee's prize apple tree. When he came out of his house, all of the boys took off running while I stood my ground. Mr. Calfee asked my name and I told him. He said he forgave me because I had not run. He told my father of the incident. My father praised me for standing and confessing my guilt, instead of condemning me for stealing the apples.

I was forbidden by my parents to cheat in school. I was one of a small minority who refrained from this practice. This training prepared me for the "honor system" I encountered when I went away to school in Virginia. I had to sign a pledge upon entering college not to cheat, and to report any cheating observed. Cheating was an offense that went before the Honor Council (composed of three teachers and three members of the student body) and would result in expulsion from school.

My father was stern and I respected his authority. He commanded much respect in the community. His word was my command. I was never whipped by hand or by thong by my father or my mother. I never heard my father say a dirty word or a "cuss" word or take the Lord's name in vain. I believe he raised me on the positive side, stressing the good points. Emphasis placed on the good in me gradually built my self-confidence.

Parents, aunt and baby (Sarah) in carriage (about 1915) standing on unpaved
Center Street off Walker, below College – Mother in big hat.

Reverend Billy

Mr. Daniel Carr acquired the property of the old academy
by trading land at the new center of the town. Two residential
streets, Center Street and Park Avenue, lined with Mr. Carr's
new houses, led to the new center of town on Mercer Street.
Formerly the turnpike to Red Sulphur Springs across the New
River in Monroe County, Mercer Street was first paved with
bricks about the time I was born. About this same time, the
Methodist Church was relocated from Main Street to the intersection of Center, Park and Mercer. Mr. Carr and company proceeded to build houses on the abandoned Academy campus. The
Carr family were leaders of the Methodist Church in the county.
The first version of the Methodist Church on Main Street had
largely been built by the personal, physical efforts of circuit
riding, Rev. Daniel Carr, uncle of the town builder.

After the railway came in 1908, Mercer Street became the
town's principal street and center of commerce. It linked the
new Virginian Railway station with the courthouse a mile away.

20

At the rail yard, a large overhead bridge carried Mercer Street across the tracks and Brush Creek, to East Princeton (first Goochville, where the Gooch family established a mill). Inhabited largely by railroad employees, East Princeton grew up as practically a separate town.

From East Princeton, the old Red Sulphur Turnpike Road went to the town of Athens. From Athens it was on to the Shanklin family's ferry on New River enroute to the Red Sulphur Springs Resort. The resort was across the river to the east in Monroe County. The Spring's three hundred-room hotel had been a popular summer resort before the Civil War.

My grandfather, the Reverend Billy Sanders, met my grandmother, Margaret Hartley, at Red Sulphur Springs. There she taught the children of her uncle, Dr. Thrasher, the spring's phy-

The Reverend Billy Sanders and his wife, Margaret Hartley, soon after their marriage. Margaret was primarily responsible for the education of their only son, Hartley, despite the meager income of her husband in the Methodist ministry.

sician. She also taught the children of the Campbell family, who owned the spring at the time.

Grandfather, a horseback circuit rider, was on his first charge in the Baltimore Conference of the Methodist Episcopal Church South. He served churches at Red Sulphur and Blue Sulphur

21

Springs and other churches in Greenbrier, Monroe and Summers counties. Reverend Billy's itinerant ministry moved among the churches of eastern West Virginia and western Virginia and Maryland.

A colored house servant, Mary, lived and moved with the family. In retirement they moved to Vinton, grandmother's girlhood home near Roanoke. Here my grandmother died and was buried. For a period after this, my grandfather, and Mary, resided with his daughter, Mrs. Nancy Sanders Gardner, in Jessup, Maryland. Here Mary died and is buried in the Gardner Family Graveyard.

My grandfather died a few years later at our home in Princeton. In his retirement he presented me, his name sake, with his gold watch and chain, which he had worn in his vest. The cover is inscribed with his (and my) initials. It is my only physical inheritance from him.

Reverend Billy's only son, Hartley, was born in Greenbrier County in 1879. One of three children, he was sent to the Methodist (Randolph-Macon) Academy at Front Royal, Virginia. For college he was sent to his father's alma mater, Randolph-Macon, at Ashland Virginia, the oldest Methodist endowed college in the country (1830). Hartley next attended the University of Virginia Law School at Charlottesville. In his last year there he roomed in Dean "Billy" Lile's home, Pavilion Ten, on the East Lawn of the University Grounds. Dean Lile told him of the opportunities in the coalfields and of the newly-formed Virginian railway which would center on Princeton.

In 1906, Hartley arrived in Mercer County, via the earlier Norfolk & Western Railway. He got off the train at Ingleside Station seven miles south of town. He rode to Princeton sitting in the seat beside the hack driver, Lewis Mathena, who offered him a drink from his flask, saying he would need it for the ride in the cold air.

Mr. Mathena eventually set up a shoe repair shop on downtown Mercer Street. There he held forth for many, many years. I often visited Lewis' shop with my father as I grew up. In those days everybody got their shoes resoled and reheeled as long as the uppers would take it and I remember often sitting in my stocking feet waiting for the new soles to be applied.

My mother's parents, George Preston Hylton and Caroline St. Clair, had come to West Virginia just before the turn of the century. Coal mining had just started in earnest. Newly-constructed railways connected the area with the coast, at Norfolk, Virginia. They moved to Bramwell from their longtime family home in the Blue Ridge Mountains of Floyd County, Virginia. Considering its small size, Bramwell was quite wealthy. Coal operators and financiers built substantial homes in Bramwell and the streets were paved with brick. Streets in the county seat were still dirt.

My grandfather became the proprietor of a large country store in this early coal mining area. He raised his family upstairs, with a large parlor on the ground floor beside the store. He also served as Justice of the Peace. Later the family moved to Princeton where my grandfather became the first county-wide assessor. He had an office at the courthouse.

My mother finished high school at Bramwell at the age of fourteen, before Princeton had its own high school. She and her brother went away to college at the Church of the Brethren (Dunkard-German Baptist) School in Daleville (near Roanoke). Their older sister attended Hollins College nearby. My mother returned to Princeton a graduate of this two-year school. She taught high school in her parents' first home near the courthouse. This was before a public high school (except for the Methodist Academy) was established.

My mother and her sister fully adopted the immersion Southern Baptist faith of their mother. Their grandmother was Sarah Jane Lee who married William Patterson St. Clair. She had been immersed as a child in Tinker's Creek at Hollins, Virginia. This baptism was performed in January by her brother Jonathan, an elder of the Enon Baptist Church. This church still stands, opposite the entrance to Hollins College. At the time of Sarah Jane Lee's childhood, what is now Hollins College was Botetourt Springs Resort. The spring house gazebo and hotel buildings are now preserved as Hollins College, the first all womens' college in Virginia. The college remains to this day exclusively female. My aunt Vera, my sister Sarah, and our daughter Katherine Todd, all attended. Katherine Todd graduated Phi Beta Kappa in 1977.

Once in Princeton, the railroad town and county seat, my mother and her sister promptly launched forth their individual soul saving Baptist careers. Virtual warfare had broken out in these hills between the Southern Baptists and all other Baptists. The Southern Baptists, and some other Baptists, had split from the original Primitive Baptist faith. Primitive Baptists were closely akin to the Dunkard, Mennonite and Amish church forms and practices.

My mother, an extraordinary beauty all her life, was exquisitely so as a young woman. My father, having just recently set himself up as a lawyer in town, and still a young bachelor, met my mother one evening as they both watched a house afire near the courthouse. Hartley immediately noticed Ina. He was smitten. That fire sparked a true love. They were soon married and for the rest of my father's life he worshipped my mother. Her love for him continued after his death in 1952 until her own in 1989, living in Katherine's and my home all but the first few years of that time.

The Colored Influence

We lived a life of relative privilege on College Hill. Until about the time I entered high school, our family had a colored cook. Her name was Fanny Evans. She was very much a part of our lives. She had an upstairs bedroom over the back porch of the house - entered off of my bedroom. At night, she told us three children ghost stories. She served as the fourth player in some games at the "carom" board until she would fall asleep in her chair and start to snore. She told us so many tales of her childhood at Lexington, Virginia, where her ex-slave mother worked in a Virginia Military Institute professor's home, that I planned to attend VMI. This was until the end of high school. Then I found out that I would never make it there with the amount of math courses required.

I think I was Fanny's favorite. If I were getting the worst of it in a neighborhood scuffle, she would come out and set matters aright. Her son, Billy, was a member of a gang of black bootleggers. He would sometimes fall prey to his buddies, who would "roll him" when he passed out drunk. Fanny would send me, alone, to the pawn shop on "the Hill" with money to get his belongings out of hock. When black boys would confront me on these missions, there was usually one or more who knew who I was and considered our family their friend. Our parents strictly instructed us never to use the word "nigger." We were told to use the word "colored" instead.

On one occasion, several colored women walked past our sandlot football field on Frederick Court on their shortcut from downtown to the Hill. I saw a roll of money lying on the ground after they passed through. I overtook the women and asked if either of them had dropped the money. One of them – Leanna Banks – claimed it as her week's salary as cook at the hospital. She had a son named William who was very strong. Some time later, I was wading in Black Lick Creek, on the western outskirts of town, with some other white boys when some black boys confronted us. William Banks stepped forward and eased the tension between the two groups.

William's mother became my law client in later days, when I wrote her will and helped her fine son with work-related injuries. My father was well known in the black community to give advice and services, often for free. Both black and white country churches often came to him to prepare the documents constituting newly-founded churches in the mountainous region, generally at little or no cost. I inherited this legacy with the black families throughout the countryside in my law practice.

While Fanny lived in a small room over our back porch, she frequently stayed weekends and other times on "the Hill" with "Aunt" Sally Bane. A path near our house passed by our sandlot on dead end Frederick Court, then undeveloped. It was used by many of the colored people, including Fanny, as a shortcut to "the Hill." Part of this shortcut went through a little valley and came out on "the Hill" by the colored Methodist Church. This secluded and wooded valley trail was a lonesome stretch for about fifty yards.

Fanny told me one time that black, peg-legged (one leg) Henry Ford, chief of the bootleg gang and the very entertaining referee at black baseball games, tried to hold her up and borrow her wage money while she walked this trail alone. Fanny pulled her folded straight razor out of the top of her dress where it had been hidden in her bosom. Henry made a clear path for her. She told me about this incident and confided that she always carried a long, folded razor when she walked alone back and forth to "the Hill." Fanny's son Billy was one of Henry "Peg" Ford's small bootleg gang.

For many years, "Peg" Ford, and a few other well-known black men, regularly loafed at the courthouse and in the alley beside the building which housed my father's office. These fellows were handy for all sorts of odd jobs. From prohibition days they ran errands for select lawyers, buying them liquor from the nearby state-owned liquor stores.

One of these courthouse regulars, Bus Hobbs, had attended Hampton Institute, one of the earliest black colleges, near the Virginia coast. He was not one of the bootleggers, but was a courthouse square habitue and enjoyed wine on a regular basis. He became one of the inner circle friends of long-time prosecuting attorney Roscoe Pendleton and lawyer Jess McCoy. They met regularly, along with Charlie Artrip, one of the town's oldest and best plumbers, in the prosecutor's office after trials, often staying into the evening, drinking and discussing criminal cases.

Jess was often in contempt of court for tardiness. He was an excellent lawyer and was especially dignified in court when he was "several sheets in the wind." Roscoe, the prosecutor, was a member of the oldest and best law family of the town. He didn't worry about his social standing. He was respected for his superior knowlege of criminal law and his skillful trial ability. His office was especially open to the lower element. He was adept in jury selections and knew exactly how the jurors evaluated the evidence. He held his elected office without any campaign advertising and, generally, without opposition.

The Hobbs family, on "the Hill," was a very singular and impressive family. The old man, Wiley Hobbs, was a very large person of about six-foot four-inches tall. He always wore bib overalls, with a coat jacket. Wiley and family had assured social standing. This was because he was the principal handyman for the Straley family, the only family in town thought to have been worth a million dollars.

During the Civil War, H.W. Straley collected taxes for the Confederacy in Mercer County, south of Flat Top Mountain. Everything north of this mountain barrier was Union. Mercer County had placed ten or twelve companies of men in the Confederate Army. During the war, Straley purchased, for Confederate money, a twenty-five-acre tract of land and home adjoining the original town along Walker Street. Our home was built in this first town addition with the Hall family graveyard partially in our backyard. After the Civil War, Straley built the first bank between Charleston, West Virginia and Bristol, Virginia, at the little town of Princeton. He bought coal mineral rights

from the settlers and sold them to the northern banking interests, who became the infamous absentee owners of West Virginia mineral deposits of coal and gas. Much of his coal rights
ended up in the Pocahontas Land Company, wholly-owned by
the Norfolk & Western Railway Company. His lawyer/banker
son inherited the impressive homeplace on Walker Street. Built
following the Civil War, after the town started to rebuild, the
home stood in a grove of ancient oaks. The large home was maintained with the help of Wiley Hobbs and other occasional colored help inside and out.

Straley Mansion of first town addition, extending Walker Street North, beyond
the Raleigh Turnpike, on land acquired from the Hall family in 1862.

Wiley Hobbs and his three sons, Bus, Herman and Jay, had
the exclusive franchise in the College Hill area to gather "slop"
from the back doors of the white residences for their hog farm
on "the Hill." It was a common sight to see the Hobbs boys coming to the back porches to collect the garbage placed there by
the white households. The white boys and Hobbs boys, with their
neighborhoods adjoining, were friends and playmates as children.

Bus Hobbs died about 1955 sitting in his rocking chair. I
attended his funeral. The black Baptist preacher, Ted Stevens,
stood up on the funeral home chapel platform and, without any
accompaniment, sang the colored spiritual, "Peace in the Valley
– there will be peace in the valley for me, some day." I was deeply

impressed. I considered Bus one of my best old family friends.

Another colored regular handyman, in the same area of the original town, was Tyler Smith. In his last years, Smith made his headquarters in Henry Deitz' store and his sleeping quarters in the Deitz' basement furnace room. Deitz' store was on lower Walker Street, near the courthouse. This store served the whole Walker Street/College Hill area by special delivery and charge account customers for more than fifty years. Just prior to his recent death at one hundred years of age, Mr. Deitz told me that he had seventy-five regular charge customers over the years who ordered by telephone and he would deliver in person. In later years, with only a few widows for charge customers, if Mr. and Mrs. Deitz didn't have the item requested, Mrs. Deitz would go to the supermarket and get the item to include in the grocery delivery. In my first years of practice, out of respect, I bought some groceries on a charge account basis from Mr. and Mrs. Deitz. Mrs. Deitz would not allow me to pay the bill completely, in order to keep me on the roster. Mr. and Mrs. Deitz would argue and converse in German or Russian inside their ancient and dimly-lit store.

Tyler Smith would kill hogs and turkeys for the whole Walker Street/College Hill neighborhood. He hunted fields and hedge rows just west of town and never wasted a shot because he knew where to find the rabbits sitting. In my early hunting days with my friend, Pete McGlothlin, on his grandfather, Dr. Wallace McClaugherty's farm at the southwest edge of town, we could always tell when Tyler had preempted the game. He sold his rabbits on the Hill as a main source of his income. Tyler would kill our Thanksgiving and Christmas turkeys and hang them upside down on the clothesline to drain, before defeathering and cooking took place. He also butchered hogs. All this was prior to World War II.

Fanny left our home when I was about twelve years of age. About the time the Great Depression began. She went to Roanoke to live with relatives. She made one or two visits to our home in the following years. On these occasions, I recall we three children were so happy to see her drop by our home. Out in front of our home we all hugged her, despite the neighbors' stares. On her visits back here, she must have stayed with her friend, "Aunt" Sally or her son, Billy, on the Hill. I believe Billy died shortly after his mother moved to Roanoke, but his good-looking wife,

Rosa Harman, continued to live for a number of years. The Will Harman family, as much white as black, was a distinguished-looking, well-respected family.

A handy supply of colored occasional laborers persisted in my area of town through my first years of practice and up until the Civil Rights days - the early 1960s. In the 1950s, when we cleared land, built and landscaped our home in the country south of town, I regularly rounded up a few hands by going to the courthouse and recruiting them.

My favorite of these day laborers was "Blue Shirt," less well known as Berryman Wood. He had come to the area from South Carolina or Georgia. He lived in a home with a former house cook at my parents' home, Anna Green. Anna's husband, Bud Green, had one leg amputated and was, thus, incapable of work. The children of that home were alternately Blue Shirts and Bud's. Blue Shirt was a favorite target of the justice of the peace system. The J.P.'s shared in the revenue fines. Poor Blue Shirt was often in jail until he paid his fine. He was skilled in many trades. He helped me sow my grass and landscape my home. He was an expert in what he called "scrubbery." He pruned fruit trees among his many trades. When he quit his work around, he gave me his long tree pruning device, which is still in my work shed. He told me he didn't need it anymore. I don't know when Blue Shirt died, he simply seemed to fade away.

We were always close to the colored families. Robert and George Hall, before the days of cinder blocks, had cut out and laid up the foundation stones of most of the first basement-built houses on College Hill. Robert's wife, Aunt Cynthia Hall, had me prepare her will in the 1960s. She paid me in two installments of brown eggs, walking about a mile from her home, in the small black settlement south of the courthouse called Augusta, to my third-floor office. In my early years of practice, when I wrote her will, I knew five generations of Aunt Cynthia's family. She was raising her great-grandson in her own home. In my present old age, I can visit either of the black Baptist or Methodist churches on the Hill and know as many old friends as I can on my visits to the downtown white churches.

After I grew up and was in the law practice myself, I would frequently encounter my former nursemaid, Jane Harris. For many years she operated the elevator in the Bluefield five-story Law & Commerce Building. She loved to tell me, and everybody

"Aunt Liza" Madison holding either me or my sister, Sarah, in our parents' first (rented) home on College Avenue next door to our landlord, Dan Carr. Our home on Walker Street was being constructed during that time.

My newspaper obituary writing on the death (about 1975) of my colored client, "Aunt Cynthia Hall." Each of these elderly, colored nurses of white family children were greatly revered by me.

Tribute Paid To Cynthia Hall

By William Sanders

"Aunt" Cynthia Hall of "Augusta" was buried yesterday.

Fifth generation Princetonian, Cynthia Hall, had six great-great-grandchildren. "A u n t" Cynthia was brought to Princeton when a girl from Pulaski by the Wilt Straley family and worked as house servant for the Straleys, the A. W. Reynolds and the Dr. (and lawyer) James W. Hale families, and for the past 20 years for the W. V. Peck family and the late "Ike" Glenn. She made her home in "Augusta" and recently gave her age as 79, although her granddaughter advises that this has been her age for at least 7 years past.

Aunt Cynthia had the greatest trust in her white friends which made you wonder if you deserved such trust and whether you were doing all you should to improve the lot of her people.

It would be difficult to find a person with a finer record of faithful employment. She was a careful manager. She had fully paid for all her burial expenses prior to her death and her will carefully provided for life estate in her granddaughter and remainder to her great-granddaughter and her great-great grandson jointly

To many residents of Princeton Aunt Cynthia seemed ageless and was much beloved and the old town will not seem quite the same without her

God rest you, Aunt Cynthia!

30

else on her elevator, of the time my mother told me I had been a bad boy. She always smiled when she repeated my reply of, "Not so bad Mama, not so bad."

A Close Family
and a Strong Father

I had a carefree boyhood. My neighborhood was my world. I walked everywhere, including to school.

To get to school, I walked down Walker Street one and one-half blocks to Douglas Street and cut across Skye Straley's vacant lot. This is where the Union soldiers killed in the Civil War battle of Princeton had been buried before they were removed to Arlington National Cemetery. On the back of this lot were two white board buildings. One of these had been the one-room, with fireplace, office of David Hall, the town's first lawyer, the other had been a one-room post office built after the Civil War. Having crossed this historic ground, I entered upon the Mercer Street School yard. This school was built in 1912 to house the first District high school on one floor and a graded school on the other floor. This fall, 1996, my grandson, Adam Sanders, will enroll as the third generation in that beautiful school building.

Mercer School.

My mother and my father were both very public people. She with her many church and club activities, and he with his law

31

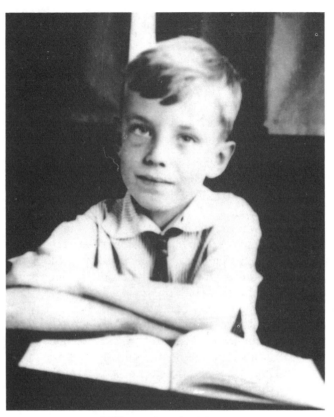

William at his school desk.

practice and political activities. My father was a person of great dignity, a statesman with a serious and intellectual turn of mind. He was a highly-principled Republican in a time and place which prized neither. He was very conservative and would strongly oppose Roosevelt and the New Deal.

Hartley had run for the office of Prosecutor of Mercer around the time of my birth. His Republican opponent, Howard B. Lee, who would later become Attorney General of West Virginia, had no car. Hartley would chauffeur his opponent to political meetings where they would then debate each other. This was the first of a number of unsuccessful campaigns for my father.

He changed from Democrat to Republican when Wilson didn't keep us out of World War I as he had promised to do. His most famous efforts would be his runs for Congress against the entrenched Kee family. Despite alcoholism and mediocrity, this family had a hold on the Congressional seat that passed from husband to wife to son. The Roosevelt New Deal welfare dole bought the votes of the coalfield community. Years later, I would take up the torch and fight this fight, also as a Republican and also without success. Hartley was one of the most prominent lawyers in Mercer County. He was the city attorney of Princeton when the town received its charter and the water and sewer services incorporated. He chartered the Bank of Athens, in that nearby town, and was their attorney all his life. He did their title and mortgage work.

He walked to work every day. His office was on the third, and top, floor of the "Law Building" (over the Straley family bank) across the street from the courthouse on the square. The town's major bank was on the ground floor. The town clock hung at the corner nearest the courthouse.

As a boy I was in awe of my father, the powerful lawyer and public figure. He was a loving and affectionate father and yet, because of the age difference or his formality, there was a certain distance between us. Much of my childhood was spent somewhat in the shadow of my glamourous and accomplished older sister Sarah. She was my father's protege. I was blissfully submerged in a boy's world of games and friendships and hunting.

My father was a very formal man. He was well known for his manner of dress. It was always, a dark blue suit, white shirt and black tie. In the summer, he sometimes wore a light gray suit with black tie and white shirt. I never saw him wear separate color trousers and jacket and never saw him wear a suit with a pattern, only solid black or navy blue and, perhaps, later in life, a thin conservative pinstripe suit. He was never seen without a jacket and tie. There is a story of a person who came to his door in the middle of the night on some emergency and before Hartley would come to the door he donned coat and tie.

To my observation, the relationship between my father and mother was a very formal one. There was a thirteen-year difference in their ages. I never heard my mother call my daddy "Hartley;" it was always "Hartley Sanders." I know this was not from lack of affection, for they loved each other devotedly.

I recall that I always said my prayers on my knees by my bed in my room. The family frequently had family prayer at supper and always when other relatives visited or we visited them in their homes. When the relatives would gather around the several homes, they would usually end up around a piano, singing hymns and other old songs. After my father's death, when my mother lived in our home, she would still play the piano and sing. Sometimes, I would join her and we would sing old songs together.

I remember Daddy had a 1927 Packard touring car with a canvas, convertible top. In the summer, the whole family would tour the countryside after supper, with the top down. It had jump seats between the front and rear seats. Two of us kids, alternately, would occupy the jump seats while the third would sulk in the back seat with Fanny, who was very happy with the back seat.

On at least two occasions, we took the Packard to Roanoke on family visits. The road was dirt the whole way. I remember a particular red clay hill at Newport, about half way to Roanoke. When wet it was impassable. There was a farmer who lived nearby who made not a little money with his team of horses pulling cars up the hill.

When I became twelve years of age, I got a .20 gauge "Fox-Sterlingworth" shotgun for Christmas. I had quail hunted with my father before that time without a gun. My father taught me safety and sportsmanship. He taught me to only shoot in your field of fire and not across your partner's front and to never cross a fence with your gun in hand, but to lay it at the post and pick it up after crossing and to keep the gun on safety until the game was seen or pointed by the bird dog.

I had a BB air rifle earlier, but was instructed never to point it at anyone and not to kill songbirds – that mostly left me with tin cans, English sparrows and starlings for targets. I got a .22 rifle about the time I got the shotgun. My closest companion then was Pete McGlothlin. (Pete later became an ace Marine fighter pilot on Guadalcanal, credited with shooting down more than five enemy planes.) We hunted the fields and woods around the outskirts of town – particularly on the south side, where Pete's grandfather, Dr. Wallace McClaugherty, had a farm. This farm was later developed as a municipal airport where Pete learned to fly an airplane. (Even later it would become a city park and hospital.) Years later, Pete told me he flew some test flights on Hawaii with Charles Lindberg toward the end of the war.

Hunting was very important to my father. Outside of our later practice of law together, it was my most important bond with him. We always had bird dogs as bird was our game. From my earliest childhood onward we kept the same bloodline of English setters. My father kept the pedigrees of his dogs more carefully than mother kept her Daughters of the American Revolution papers. While I was off to war, my favorite dog, Count Mojawk, I had personally trained, was killed by a car. The fact was kept from me until I came home and was greeted by an almost duplicate of old Count, his son Prince, choice of litter received as stud fee.

I remember when my father abandoned golf and took up setter bird dogs and quail hunting. I was about twelve years old. Before that time, he had hunted with a setter named "Low Mohawk," who may have been jointly owned or passed around among the fellow hunters. Low was the best around. He pointed the birds by sitting down, which was not the classic style, but he was steady on the point and, when he sat down, you could be sure he had the birds.

An Englishman named Llewellyn had developed a very purt strain of English setter dogs. This strain fascinated my father.

A new Baptist preacher from Tennessee named Reverend Ogle moved to town. He was quite a setter bird dog fancier and became a good friend of my father. I remember that my father bought a Llewellyn Setter through the preacher. The dog was named "Hall's Ringallo Jack." The price paid was $250.00, an astronomical sum of money.

I took Jack under my special care. He was a wonderful dog. He was very gentle. All the family fell in love with Jack. In the field, he ranged widely, with great style, and would hold a point 'til you found him.

We bread Jack to the old "Mohawk" line of local setter dogs. We got the choice of the litter and named him "Count Mojawk." He was registered accordingly.

Old Jack and I, together, trained "Count" in fields around the town. If Count flushed the birds and failed to hold the point, I made sure he received a reprimand if I had to chase him over hill and dale to do it. He got the message. If he was inclined to steal the point from Jack, rather than back up Jack's point, Jack would give him a low growl and warn him. Jack and I made Count the acknowledged best bird dog in the area.

I had numerous great hunts with Jack and Count and, when my father couldn't go, Pete McGlothlin and I would take the two dogs hunting on all sides of the town, most often by walking from our homes on College Hill via shortcuts on the north, west and south of the town to the bird fields and hillsides and woods. We acquired an amazing knowledge of the quail habitat around our town which is, today, grown up with sprawling subdivisions, hospitals and various development.

I recall the day we lost old Jack. My father and I were hunting out in the open country of tall hills and deep and wide valleys. It was getting late and we wanted to bring in the dogs and put them in the car and go home. Jack was way across a wide valley. His hearing must have gone bad. We called and used our whistles and he seemed to go the opposite way, like he was answering our echoes. It got dark, and we went home without Jack. We came back for days to inquire throughout miles of neighborhood, but could never find old Jack. That was a sad time just as I was entering college.

My career as a lawyer may have been set in motion in the fifth grade when my teacher, Mr. Alonzo Clark, cast me in the role of Scrooge in the Christmas play. He bragged on me for speaking out clearly my one line, "Bah, humbug" throughout the play. This gave me confidence in speaking out loud and clearly, whether before a class, in marine training or any public speaking. Mr. Clark opened our class the first thing in the morning by having all of us standing and singing his favorite hymn, "Rock of Ages." He would often tell us a bear or panther story before getting down to work with the lessons.

Sarah

Sarah (December 24, 1915-October 1934), my beautiful sister, was only a year and two months my elder but she was always so far above me in maturity and attainments that it was as if we lived in different worlds. As the first child, she was my father's favorite. She became my father's protege and had the intellect to absorb his teachings. He coached her in the classics, public speaking and debating. In public school she was always at the top of her class. She read all the books in Daddy's library;

Sarah and her most persistent boyfriend,
Randolph Pendleton in high school graduation gowns.

Plutarch's Lives, the Harvard Classics, *Abbott's World History*, etc. She was highly popular among her peers. She shone. Sarah won every distinction and honor.

I, on the other hand, was living in a sort of awkward juvenile haze that is unique to young boys. I had grown tall but was thin and ungainly. I was too skinny for team sports and I was no scholar. I had my own concerns with which I was absorbed; chief among them was hunting. However, I was editor of the high school newspaper, *The Pinnacle*.

I had been held back one year in school, along with the rest of my class, due to a first grade teacher who taught us fairy tales rather than academic subjects. As a result, Sarah was several years ahead of me in school.

Sarah had, at an early age, developed into an outstandingly beautiful girl with mature feminine qualities. Needless to say, she attracted a wide following of young men, many of them several years older than she. One particular suitor was Randy Pendleton. He was the son of wealthy attorney John R. Pendleton, a friend of my father and, with my father, one of the most prominent lawyers in Princeton. Randy had a fancy car, a powerful and sporty roadster. That car had an especially musical horn. At night after he had left Sarah at home, I could hear him blowing the horn as he drove away, a musical goodnight to my sister. Randy had a jealous and possessive nature. He was focused on

Sarah. He would employ other local boys and with them attempt to discourage any would-be out-of-town suitors. Other local suitors included Price Dyer, Gordon Todd, Harry Waugh, Steve Meem and Paige Woolridge, all of whom became outstanding citizens.

Sarah graduated from high school with honors. Daddy's fortunes had been devastated by the Great Depression. He was slowly recouping. Somehow he managed to send Sarah to Hollins College near Roanoke, Virginia, our Aunt Vera's alma mater. Sarah had a great first year at Hollins. She had made a wonderful academic record and had been elected to be vice president of next year's sophomore class. She returned to Princeton and home for the summer of 1934. She was nineteen.

It was late summer when Sarah went on a hayride down Oakvale mountain to a swimming hole with many of her friends. An old lawyer, Henley French Day, who could barely see and whose eyes seemed to dance in his head, was driving his old car from a side road, almost running into the truck full of young people. Sarah was sitting beside her date, Price Dyer the football hero, on the tailgate of the truck with her feet dangling. Sarah was thrown from the truck when driver Danny Flanigan swerved to avoid a crash. She fractured her skull and broke her hip in her fall.

I was home alone that day. Mother and Daddy were away in Roanoke and younger sister Caroline was at a friend's. I received a phone call that Sarah was injured and was being taken to the hospital. Sarah was taken to Dr. Todd's Memorial Hospital in Princeton. She was placed in traction and after some time placed in a lower body cast. Her many adoring friends covered her cast in signatures and messages.

She appeared to be making an appropriate recovery and was released to come home, in bed. In late September she developed peritonitis, a serious infection of the intestines. Sulfa drugs had been recently discovered but the news of this discovery had not reached Princeton. Sarah began to sink and had to be re-admitted to the hospital. I can still remember the terrible feeling that came over me as I watched the ambulance take her away.

One evening in October Sarah sent word for me to come to her hospital bedside. When I arrived she affected a light and breezy manner to allay my obvious concern. She joked about my dating a certain girl and generally conversed with me in a casual way. Before I left she told me to "carry on." This was the last time I would ever see her.

The next night, near my bedtime, I was inside the house which was filled with family and friends. I got an urge to be alone and walked out onto the front porch. Once alone on the porch I felt such a strong sense of Sarah's presence. Looking back on it I am sure this was the moment of her death. At that moment I felt, and I still believe, that there was a spiritual transference from Sarah to myself. I have never experienced anything to match the power of that experience. From that moment forward my life was changed. When I returned indoors I learned that a phone call had been received telling of Sarah's death. Mother and Daddy were at her bedside when she died.

As she died Sarah sang the words of a then current popular song; "I saw stars, I heard an angel sing, the moment I fell for you."

Mother and Daddy were crushed by Sarah's death. They both aged noticeably. The community was in shock. Sarah had been a popular and outstanding young woman. Her death was treated as a major tragedy. The funeral was held at the First Baptist Church where the crowd and flowers overflowed. Friends from the area as well as from colleges in Virginia attended.

Hartley Loses All in Great Depression

Sarah's death came in the midst of the Great Depression. When she died we were still living in our house on Walker Street. We would not live there much longer. These were sad times for many. My father had become over-extended during the late 1920s with investments and bank loans to fund his speculation. The crash and the subsequent desperate years saw him lose all. He went bankrupt. His white-columned Walker Street pavillion, my childhood home, was lost.

By the late 1930s the family would be living in rented quarters again. The family moved one block up Walker Street to the former home of Rev. Eugene Blake. Reverend Blake had been the headmaster of the old academy and his home was a large brick edifice.

The Blake home, and other wonderful properties, had been bought up by Dr. I.T. Peters, a coal company doctor from Mayberry in adjoining McDowell County. Dr. Peters had a steady income and was a superb poker player. It was rumored that one night he broke James Elwood Jones, the rich coal operator who lived in a mansion on the hilltop overlooking Mayberry Camp.

College

In a way, Sarah's death made it possible for me to attend college. I don't think Daddy could have afforded to send two children to college at that time.

In 1936, Daddy took me to be enrolled at his, and his father's, alma mater, Randolph-Macon. I could not have received a scholarship based on my lackluster performance in high school. Daddy didn't think that I should work but should rather concentrate on my studies. He scraped together all his resources to pay for my years at Randolph-Macon and law school that would follow.

My Father the Lawyer

My father walked to work each morning down North Walker Street. Most of the first lawyers of the town lived along this street and walked to their offices near the courthouse.

Most of the town's lawyers, including my father, had their offices on the top two floors of the Princeton Bank, built by the Straley family on the corner across from the Mercer County Courthouse. The building had a stairwell from the ground floor which rose to wide central halls on the second and third floors. The lawyers' offices on these floors faced out on the hall and stairwell emerging in the middle. Most of the lawyers kept their doors open onto the hall and the secretaries knew every other lawyer's clients and business by the coming and going to their doorways.

My father's office was at the front of the top floor and the last door to come to in the whole building. He kept his door shut. His clients either came to the office by prearrangement or by rejection by one or more of the other offices, whose clients wandered in, not knowing which lawyer they would choose until they got in the building and took their pick.

My Father's Understudy

I attended court sometimes to see my father's trials. I even went to Washington once with my father to see him introduced to the U.S. Supreme Court. At an interlude, my father motioned for me to come up to the Bar of the Court, where he introduced me to Chief Justice William Howard Taft. At this time, Justice Taft had already served as President of the United States. I was a skinny ten or twelve year old. Justice Taft must have weighed three hundred pounds or more. His black robe made him seem enormous. The elevated bench made it all the more overpowering. The justice leaned over the high bench and I put my hand up higher than my head to shake his hand, which

41

seemed to be as large as a ham. I recall my father later getting President Taft's son, Senator Robert Taft, to come to speak at our local annual Lincoln Day Republican Banquet.

Hartley and the Case of White Slavery

Just before going off to college, I attended a week-long trial in the Federal District Court in Bluefield. I watched my father and his co-counsel, ex-Judge Howell Tanner, defend the Mayor of the Town of War, McDowell County, West Virginia, in the heart of the coalfields, on a charge of white slavery. The mayor was charged with procuring and transporting across state lines certain prostitutes to ply their ancient trade in his town.

The trial was before Judge McClintock, famous for his war on moonshiners. The super-righteous judge obviously wanted to make an example of Mayor Brown. Mr. Brown was from a fine old farming family in rural Summers County. Several generations of his family owned and lived at the old Methodist Brown's Chapel in a beautiful countryside setting – which was probably the connection that brought about my father's employment in the case. It seemed the judge rode the back of my father, who was chief defense counsel, all through the trial. I was amazed how my father kept calm in all of the harsh rulings and comments of the judge.

A crowded, standing-room-only courtroom heard the jury announce its verdict, "not guilty." A roar of applause rose from the crowd. Judge McClintock banged the bench with his gavel repeatedly to obtain order. He then directed the U.S. Marshall to bring a certain fat man standing at the back wall forward before him. The man was declared in contempt and ordered to pay a $50 fine or go to jail. My father and Judge Tanner paid the man's fine on the spot.

I recall I was not too young to appreciate that the young women prostitutes were right good-looking female specimens. One after another they testified that they were volunteers and that Mayor Brown did not procure them. I believe, in retrospect, the girls had been well rehearsed by defense counsel, an ex-judge and a dignified Methodist preacher's son, my father.

This trial was an indelible lesson to me in court decorum.

Respect for the court is a paramount principle – the court represents the very institution of the English Common Law, coming down to this nation from the Magna Carta. My father was a model of respect for the court, however unfair or biased the court's rulings may have been. At the same time, my father carefully taught me and showed me by his conduct to always make and preserve the record of evidence and rulings to save the inalienable right of appeal to a higher court. Many are the times when an intolerable judge has unsuccessfully tried to keep me from vouching and preserving the record of the evidence upon his adverse rulings during the progress of trials.

COLLEGE
AND LAW SCHOOL

College Life

I left home for my first year of college in 1936. My father went with me on the train to Richmond and then to Randolph-Macon at Ashland, just north of Richmond. He remained with me at the college several days. It was his first visit back since he left the college about 1904. He boarded the train for home and

William at college with sideburns applied by charcoal and wearing his college letters, earned as a member of the tennis team.

his last words to me were, "Put studies first and, if you don't run with the best crowd, run alone." I took his advice on the second program, the social part of the formula, but reversed the first part about studying, that is, until I arrived at law school, where I played catch up on the studying part.

I failed first-year math. I excused my failing grade to my father by telling him over half of the class failed with me. He indelibly impressed me by his indignant reply. He told me I would never get anywhere or become anything by comparing myself with those of inferior attainment. He also told me if I did not want to continue in college, he would buy me a truck and I could drive a truck for a living. I got the message. I remember that as one of the several landmark lessons from my father, whose practice was always equal to his preachment. He did not preach much, but he found the right times and places to turn me in the right direction. I often remember this and his several other guideposts.

I have read the lives of Jefferson and Washington. They were two very different people, except that they both loved the land, as I do. I observe that their lives were regulated, in part, by maxims and rules of conduct. My father's maxims helped me. I have often thought of his admonitions. I applied them in various endeavors, even in trivial matters such as games. For example, as I tried to become a better tennis player I sought opponents better than I was, instead of those who didn't take the game seriously. This is the same kind of advice he gave me when he told me at college to have no friends if I didn't have good friends. His words and advice guided me all along. When I was too skinny to play high school football I wanted to go out for manager of the team. He advised against it saying that was a job for a hired hand. When I was very young, I fell in with some boys who gathered around a smoldering fire of a restaurant near the courthouse, which had burned to the ground the night before. We were scavenging through the ashes and coming up with coins and trinkets, when my father appeared on the scene and called me aside and scolded me severely.

At college, my extracurricular activites remained on a par with my earlier College Hill neighborhood promotions. I became the first, and probably last, president of my fraternity to attain that post in his second year. My fraternity had won the scholarship cup among the six social fraternities on the campus for twenty-five straight years. Perhaps, my social proclivities gave the fraternity a little balance among their fraternity peerage.

The editorship of the school newspaper had belonged to my fraternity for several years. I was interested in journalism as a career. My junior year I was grooming myself in full expectation that the job of editor would be mine as a senior. The Board of Publication, consisting of three faculty and three students, offered me the post. However, they attached a condition. They reserved the right of the Board, or any of their three faculty members, to censor my editorials. I declined the post under those terms. When it came time to announce the next editor, a sports reporter was named. I was devastated! I remember walking around in a daze. After this, I applied for entrance to law school right out of my junior year. This event committed me to a law career and allowed me to complete my three-year law course just in time for World War II. Kind providence at work.

To qualify for law school with only three years college, I was required to have completed two years of Latin. On my final exam, I needed at least a seventy-nine percent grade to bring my first semester grade up to the passing level of seventy-five. I wrote a note on my final exam paper that I intended to go to law school and needed a passing grade to do so. Dr. Bowen awarded the grade of seventy-nine, I believe, by his good graces and his acquaintance with both my grandfather and father before me.

Boy-Girl Relationship

Girl consciousness came into my existence in the last year of high school. The girls would set up parties at their homes. The boys in my neighborhood were somehow inveigled into playing bridge with the girls at these parties. That started the erosion. Pretty soon, the girls taught the boys to dance and that was the end of our separate boys' world.

Girl consciousness became the main course when I entered college. Although I went to a boys' college the subject of girls and how to pursue them on weekends dominated our thinking and planning. At least, this was the case with six social fraternities of my day.

Money was something children in school did not need and did not have except for some few nickels in pockets for candy and monies on Saturday mornings when movies were mostly cowboy and Indians and admission cost ten cents to a quarter – a hot dog was five cents for many years. The same frugality carried over into college, with those families who could afford to send their children to college.

Most of the colleges in Virginia were all boy or all girl. The practice grew for the girls and the boys to invite each other to their separate schools for weekend dances. The girls coming from their schools in buses (with chaperons). The girls knew when to leave the dance to go to the boarding homes where they were put up. The boys would somehow get to the girls' school dances by loading up on any and sundry old jalopies they could scrounge up.

All of the years I went to college and to law school, I mostly hitch-hiked back and forth to home on school breaks. I sometimes went back and forth on the train from Bluefield when my finances were up. Christmas and semester breaks of the boys' and girls' schools coincided and a lot of visiting around on the trains took place.

My money allowance was slim and none of the boys had money to burn. Very few had cars. "Doc" Register, an older and very settled fraternity "brother" at college, had a black A Model Ford with rumble seat. He was the exception among us and never thought there was but one girl in the world, Juliana Hartsock, who lived right by the campus with her widowed mother. The rest of the boys in the fraternity looked on her as a big sister and she was immune to any advances by any of us lesser, more freewheeling members of the club. We got a lot of service out of Doc's old Ford with running boards and rumble seat.

In college, for the most part, the boys and the girls played the field. Our dates at the dances were introduced to all of our friends and our friends danced with our dates and the dances were generally termed break dances, when the idea was not to get "stuck" too long with any girl. The prettier girls and the better dancers had lines of fellows waiting for their turn to dance. We were proud to have a date who was popular with all. If you didn't dance with your friend's date, he was slighted and it was great credit to bring the prettiest and the best dancers as dates for the weekend dances and parties.

In the southern schools, a bold practice by the most daring boys and girls grew up – late dating. This was a secretive process of one fellow making a secret arrangement with another friend or rival's date to meet her after her date took her home and took his leave. One of my friends in law school from Charleston, South Carolina, spoke a dialect called "geetchy." He was woefully unsuccessful in his persistent attempts at late dating. The girls couldn't understand his language in asking for a "let det."

I recall my classmate, Joe Massie, of Winchester, Virginia, had Tyler Wilson and me as his house guests on the long weekend of the "Annual Apple Blossom Festival." Joe's sister attended a private girls' school in Pennsylvania. She had a couple of her schoolmates as her houseguests. This practice in our time was called a house party and, of course, it required a pretty good size house. We boys carried the girls to several parties around the community and, after the big dance of the occasion, we brought the girls home and then we three boys, Joe included, slipped out to seek the company of other girls elsewhere. I can't recall whether we acquired dates or whether we just went forth looking – I believe the latter.

When we got back to Joe's big house, Mrs. Massie had locked the door and all of the others were bedded down tight. Dressed in our tuxedos and tails, we outfoxed Joe's mother, by climbing up on the roof of the porch and entering the second-story window rather than awaken anybody and be confronted with our irregular activities. Stern Mrs. Massie respected our ingenuity and no one acted any wiser at the breakfast table.

The summary of all of this growing up process is that "going steady" was practically unheard of unless you were going to retire from life and give up all of the frivolity that was a necessary relief from studying and acquiring an education. Meeting people was no problem, boys or girls. We loved them and left them until the time was right to start earning our own livings. When that time grew close, we zeroed in on our favorite girl for the long haul.

This social order was completely changed and a new generation of children were without this freedom of mixing and mingling and finding permanent life partners. The open social order of my day was gone with the wind of Vietnam distrust and dissent. We are proud that none of our four children who came along in the totally different Vietnam era chose to join fraternities at their colleges, which had become much more promiscuous than our pre-war social activities had been. In our day, we became acquainted with each other by family and schooling background. In the post-war world, such provincialism was a thing of the past. When we met a new girl, it didn't take long to find mutual friends and kindred. In yet older days, in the Virginias, a lot of cousins married cousins, true in all ranks of the social order – it grew out of such familiarity that boys and girls were able to freely communicate in my college days. It was a smaller world then.

WARFARE

Going to War Via New Zealand

After my father put me through his college (which had been his father's college) and his beloved University of Virginia Law School, World War II reared its ugly head in the land. I thought most seriously of becoming a "conscientious objector." My inclination was anything but military. The Methodist Church philosophy at the time was pacifist. I felt that no war was ever really won and that the flower of youth was always sacrificed on the alter of war. My own war experience confirmed this fact to me. The best and the bravest died and we lesser ones came back home. Had my war been the later Vietnam War, I am sure I would have refused to serve.

The subject was vigorously debated at a family dinner in our home not long before I signed up for the marine corps. My mother's soul saving sister and her husband, the choir director, were having dinner with us. My uncle had come from a large family, but he and my aunt had no children, having lost two children in infancy. I took the conscientious objection position and my uncle took the go-to-war position. My father stayed on the sideline.

My birth date was February 1917, and my sister Sarah's was 1915. My father, with two children, was exempted from World War I and, instead, was active in certain patriotic war support programs locally – a "Four Minute Man," making war support speeches. When Woodrow Wilson campaigned to keep us out of that war and, as soon as elected got us into the war, my father changed his old south Democratic party registration to that of the Republican party, whereupon one of his good-looking female cousins told him "never darken my door again." I was aware my father felt World War I was not our war and that we should not have become involved.

In my last year of law school, 1942, Lew Brundage, a student from Wyoming State, and I decided to go to Washington, DC, and sign up for the Marine Corps Officer Training Program and obtain a deferment until our graduation that year.

Virginia schools still trained many West Virginia lawyers. Mountainous terrain and poor roads made it difficult to travel to West Virginia's only law school in the northern end of the state, until the advent of modern transportation. The main roads were still the original settlement roads, running east and west.

The railways were, likewise, oriented. Lawyers not trained in the old Virginia schools were self-taught by reading law in the older lawyer's offices. That was the flavor of the local profession when I joined it in 1948, with several of the best lawyers still around who had merely read law and then passed the bar without a formal law school education.

I went to law school in the coat-and-tie days at the University of Virginia. My roommate, Bob Gwathmey of Hanover Court House, had also been at Randolph-Macon. The dean of the law school was Frederick Dean Gordon Ribble, the son of an Episcopal minister. He called Bob and me to his office to read us a letter he had received from the new dean of Randolph-Macon. This new dean had been our math professor. He had been famous for flunking over half of his students. He was a contemporary of my father in college and they had corresponded during my struggle to conquer his math classes. The dean's letter to the law school stated that Gwathmey was a serious student but that there was not much hope for me.

The law dean, with his liberal Episcopalian background, was amused by the letter. Happily, I was safely beyond the required math courses of college days. Bob and I both made it through and both finally made small town country lawyers. He later became a judge in old Hanover Court House near Richmond, Virginia. After law school, he joined the navy and served on a mine sweeper in Norfolk harbor for the war's duration. I went forth to the marines.

College or law school photo, showing what I looked like when the Marine Training Camp First Sgt. said I was the most disgusting sight he had ever seen and promptly sent me off for a haircut.

Upon graduation from law school, I got on a train and ended up in

Quantico, Virginia. I arrived at boot camp, a green recruit, with wavy blond hair and a silly grin on my face. I was the product of a sheltered small town background. Also, I had been a "legacy" student in a provincial college and law school. Even with my law degree, I was unimpressive as an officer candidate. The training lasted for ten weeks, with another ten weeks as a second lieutenant in Officer's School in Quantico.

The officer's candidate training was a fast and furious ten weeks. My platoon sergeant was about the coarsest and ugliest man I had ever met. He and the first sergeant of the Tenth Candidate's Class set about to wipe the grin off my pink and shining face. I don't remember either of their names. I do recall another platoon sergeant of the training company named Kelly. he was a red-haired friendly person who came up to me after the corps decided to keep me. He congratulated me on staying with the program despite the riding I got from the other two. He offered his home as shelter for my date, who was coming up for the ceremonies and dance.

I was in the lower part of the class and my military bearing was nothing to brag about. However, I had a good voice to give commands and count cadence. Also, I was one of six, out of more than a one hundred in my company, to qualify as Expert on the rifle range. Some of the better physical specimens had no "command presence" or had squeaky voices. Another lawyer, my good friend Tony Scariano, from Chicago, was class jester. He kept us all highly amused by mimicking the officers and sergeants behind their backs. He had served on the police force in Washington, DC, while he was going through law school and had served as an aide to Illinois Senator Lucas prior to signing up for the marines. Unfortunately, he failed out because he was flat-footed. His feet made him fall behind on the vigorous hikes, whereas, my feet were the best constructed part of my, otherwise unimpressive, anatomy. We kept up correspondence throughout the war. He served as a captain in the intelligence section of the United States Fifth Army in Italy. He was decorated. His knowledge of Italian made him very useful in winning the war on the Italian front.

Everything was alphabetical in the Quantico program. In ranks and bunks, it was Sanders, Santilli and Savelle. Santilli was a large tackle on the Fordham football team and Savelle, from the Bayous of Louisiana, was a tall professional baseball player. Alec Santilli was later killed on Saipan Island and I visited his grave there. Both of these men were strapping marines. I was traveling in very safe company. We took our liberties together in DC, a short trip from our base, at least when I wasn't grounded for failing to look or behave like a marine. Once I was grounded by some sharp-eyed colonel for "oggling the girls" who passed our ranks going to secretarial jobs in the headquarters building. My big buddies kept me safe from disagreeable encounters with other servicemen playing the "liberty field" around the streets and bars of the nation's capitol.

I received my orders in December 1942, sending me to a replacement staging camp near San Diego. I was given a few days delay to spend Christmas at home with family. My sister Caroline had already married my college roommate, John Douglas Sterrett, of Monterey, in Highland County, Virginia. They were at an army training base where he was an army tank officer.

Before leaving to go back to the service, a few days after Christmas, my father called us together by the piano in the little music room, a room with a piano and a lot of windows next to the carport on the side of the house. Standing there together, in a huddle, we said the 23rd Psalm. My father drove me to the train station ten miles away. Standing there in uniform on the station platform, as we parted company to board the train, I kissed my father goodbye, just as I had kissed my father goodnight or goodbye to college, all of my life – on the lips. I would have never remembered this routine act at the train station had it not been recalled years later when my father mentioned that a friend of his, Sally Sanders Evans (of an unrelated Bluefield family), saw us from a distance. She later told him that she was impressed by this act upon my departure for the Pacific War Zone. Kissing hello and goodbye in this fashion had always been a custom in our family whenever members and cousins met among both my father and my mother's families. Any close relative who turned their cheek and did not kiss me on my mouth made me feel that such relative was a little less than genuine and that I did not have his or her full approval.

I boarded the train and several days later ended up in California. I spent the next two weekends dancing to the Harry James Orchestra at the Coconut Grove in Los Angeles. My date was a fair young maiden of Scripps College whom I had met on the

58

train ride west. She was real pretty, but the war has eclipsed her name.

We received orders that sent us closer to the theater of war. It took us about thirty days by ship zig-zagging to avoid submarine torpedoes to arrive in Wellington, New Zealand. We were replacements for the fallen officers of the Second Division of marines. The Second Marines were reassembling gradually in the Wellington area. Their ranks had been devastated in crippling experiences at Guadalcanal, in the Solomon Islands.

Enroute to New Zealand, we stopped briefly at New Caladonia to help build a tent camp beside the Catholic Church Mission of St. Louis. I wandered "off limits" through the native grass hut village with the natives peeking out as I passed. I traveled seven thousand miles and thought I should see this oddity, despite the off-limits sign, installed to prevent all of the troops from swarming into the village and scaring the natives to death. I remember seeing an albino child in this otherwise pure black Micronesian community. New Caladonia, owned by the French, had served as a French penal colony in earlier years.

Upon landing at Wellington Harbor in New Zealand, and before assignment to a unit, I was given the duty of assisting a marine captain in the burial of two or three marines who had died enroute from Guadalcanal. The captain showed up inebriated and fairly useless. I had to take charge without any real knowledge of such affairs. The Quantico course had not covered funerals. I was there with a small assemblage of marines and some local citizens. It was at the funeral home or church, I can't remember which. At the adjoining cemetery, after the firing of the volleys and taps by the bugler, it was discovered the graves were not dug quite wide enough to enable the lowering of the coffins. I had to hail the New Zealand grave digging squad hovering nearby. With their spades they shaved off the inside walls of the graves to conclude the burial. Thus was the beginning of my service in the Pacific Theater War.

I was soon assigned a platoon of Quadalcanal veterans in the weapons company (D for Dog Company) of the First Battalion, Second Regiment of the Second Division of the United States Marine Corps (D-1-2). They were setting up their tent camp on the upper, mountainous, east side of the road and railway at McKays Crossing. The rest of the division was encamped in this general area, which included the Sixth and Eighth regiments and Headquarters Regiment with all attached troops. The main body of troops was located in a big sprawling encampment half-way between Paraparumu (Paraparam, for short) and the rail station of Paekokarika (Paekok, for short). From Paekok we would catch the narrow gauge train to Wellington, the capitol

Map of Wellington area.

city.

I was introduced as a fresh officer, with no combat experience, to my platoon of malaria-ridden veterans at a battalion

60

formation in a cow pasture on a hillside above the tent encampment. Upon inspection of the platoon, I nervously handed the first man in the first rank's rifle to him backwards. He refused to take it until I reversed the weapon. The rest of the platoon were barely able to suppress their amusement. When the officers departed the field, the platoon was dismissed by Platoon Sgt. John Bowler, who told them to fall out and meet him in his tent immediately. Once in his tent he told them, in very clear terms, if he ever heard anyone mention the event at camp or on liberty, he would deal with him accordingly. Therefore, the matter was forgotten. That was certainly a humble beginning of my active service in the war zone, and my esteem with the men had to go up because it couldn't go any lower.

We spent nine months in New Zealand. My quarters were in a row of small wooden shanties on a hillside above the tent camp of the troops. There was enough room to walk between two cots, with a kerosene stove and a window at the end of the building at the head of the cots and a door at the other end at the foot of our cots. My roommate was the remarkable Corbin West, the best poker and crap player among the officers of the battalion. Corbin was proud to have been a hobo on the railroads all over America before joining the Marine Corps. That made him an instant hero to me for weekend liberty.

The New Zealand boys were away on the shores of North Africa and, with the British, were serving as shock troops fighting Field Marshall Rommel and his Nazis. We marines took it as our patriotic duty, and part of the war effort, to comfort the young women left behind. Thus occupied, most of the officers spent their weekends in Wellington or running around on extended leaves all over the north and south of those two beautiful islands, in company with the New Zealand girls.

On most weekends, the Second Division camp became largely deserted. My weekend habitat, along with most of the other officers, was downtown Wellington. It was not uncommon to see marines and their girlfriends carrying groceries to a home or apartment for a very domestic weekend together.

Corbin and I maintained a large room with a fireplace in a boardinghouse in the center of Wellington. Except for us, the boardinghouse was occupied entirely by New Zealand girls working for the government. Corbin attained another sort of hero status one night when he slipped into the room of two girls and slept in the same bed with them. Mrs. Brown, the harried landlady, lived in the house. A very pretty girl, named Mary Cameron, assisted Mrs. Brown in keeping the house in order. Shortly after I arrived home in late 1945 after the war's end, Mary called me on the long-distance telephone from New Zealand to see if I was alright.

Our nine month sojourn in New Zealand left me with many memories. Our favorite fastfood was the "fish-n-chips" sold at corner stands. The "fish" was the wonderful whitefish so abundant in the cold waters of New Zealand. New Zealand also had a great abundance of sheep. The wool was sent half-way around the world, to England, to be manufactured into cloth. Thus preserving the superior economy of the mother country.

The New Zealand girls all spoke of England as "home." We teased them about this because they had never "beeen" there, and probably never would. Most New Zealanders, when they parted company with one another, would say, "Cheerio!" Their movie houses seemed to get only second-rate, dull British humor films. At the movie's conclusion, everyone would stand up and sing "God Save the King." (We Americans know the tune from grade school as "My Country Tis of Thee," which ends with the words *great God, our King.*)

The seasons around Wellington were either wet or dry. The temperature was such that central heat was not the rule. We always slept under blankets, since the weather was not extreme but simply uncomfortable. It seemed that bathing was done sparingly and their bathrooms were rigged with "water closets," their term for a toilet, and where a reservoir of water was installed in the wall above the washing facilities and toilet. We got the impression that water should be conserved because of all this rigging. The people ate mutton and more mutton, but not many green vegetables. Accordingly, many of the young girls had false teeth.

Regardless of these rugged, and sometimes primitive, aspects of life "down under," the hospitality and genuine freindship of these wonderful people was rare. We marines became very attached to the place. Friendliness was the common tie between us. We were in this war together, buddies or "cobbers," despite small differences. We were all commoners and we overlooked their worship of the Royal House of England. The people of New Zealand took us into their homes and hearts. They saw us as their saviors from an imminent Japanese invasion that would have taken place, had we not come halfway around the world to prevent it. We became the New Zealand Marine Corps. When the battle of Tarawa took place, shortly after our New Zealand stay, casualty lists were posted publicly in Wellington. Citizens gathered in large crowds, anxiously looking for the names of their sweethearts and friends.

My parting gesture to New Zealand had been in the form of a date with my best girlfriend, Betty. Our flotilla of ships lay at anchor in Wellington Harbor for a few days. We were on stand-by and forbidden to go ashore. Nevertheless, I went ashore on the last evening before we were to leave for the theater of war. I met Betty at the docks. We walked to a nearby air raid shelter. There we found a degree of seclusion on the concrete steps leading down to the locked shelter. It is amazing how young lovers can make do in unusual circumstances and tight quarters.

Returning to the dockside late that evening, I found the steel, wovenwire fence closed tight. Frantically, I somehow managed to climb the twelve-foot high fence. I searched and located a single sailor. As luck would have it, he was the coxswain of a small boat, my ship captain's gig. This good fellow saved me. He agreed to take me back to the ship. We shipped out for the war in the morning. With that evening's romantic adventure, I had nearly missed my first campaign of the war. This would have meant total disgrace. Kind providence was still at work.

Many months later, from Hawaii, I sent Betty a ring with some kind of precious stone in it. It wasn't a diamond. We did not otherwise correspond after New Zealand. I had never met her family, who lived in a town halfway up the North Island. I am sure they were wonderful people. I guess Betty knew I had other girlfriends, but I am sure she knew she was my best girlfriend at the time.

My happy social campaign in New Zealand came to an abrupt halt when we shoved off for an unknown destination.

Our destination was not announced until a few days before we landed at Betio Island. This was the largest atoll in the Tarawa Group of the Gilbert Islands in the middle of the world's biggest ocean. It was 21 November 1943. The island that greeted us was home to a Japanese airfield and was surrounded by extensive fortification facing out to sea in all directions. After all the waiting, I was now about to enter the real war.

WAR
IN THE
CENTRAL PACIFIC

Tarawa

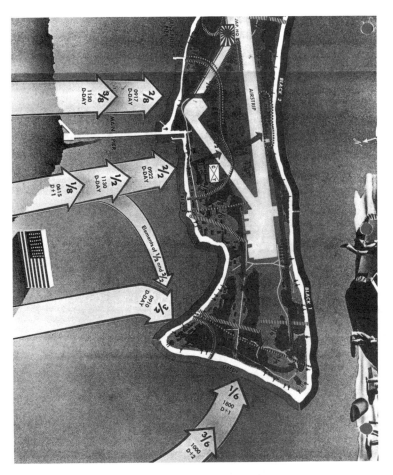

Diagram of Betio Atoll in the Tarawa group of Gilbert Islands in the central Pacific showing the Second Marine units' landing areas and the pier at the junction of Red Beach one and two. Connected pillboxes where I directed my efforts were located several hundred feet to the right (north) of the pier where the beach curved inland and at the point of a long rectangular pillbox built into the sea wall. This strong point caused great havoc to the landing forces and, especially, those of the Eighth Marines on the second morning.

At daybreak, we watched an awesome bombardment from the ship's deck. The Destroyers of our floatilla, assisted by fighter/bombers, pounded the small island of Betio (code named *Helen* in our war plans). The Grumman small marine bombers and strafers and the Navy SBD gull winged dive bombers stole the show by their direct bombing of the island's fortifications. Several of the SBD dive bombers failed to come out of their dives and flew directly into their targets.

Then we began the long process of disembarkation. By rope nets hanging over the sides of the ships, we descended into Higgin's boats in the water below. I encountered Lt. Justin Mills, a platoon leader in "C" Company and one of the better poker players in the battalion officer's mess. He was a "Canal" veteran from Texas. He would often sing a sad little ditty about "the long steel rails and the short cross ties - it's a long way back home." He said he felt it was too bad I had to go ashore into the hell that lay ahead, but he told me he was ready for it. Within days, his body was found, face down, in front of a Japanese pillbox. (One of our "D" Company Squad Sergeants, Abbott, a Mormon from Utah, who carried his Mormon Bible in his pack, was also found lying face forward in front of a pillbox opening.)

Corbin West was also a "C" Company Platoon Leader. However, after we left the ship in our landing boats, I didn't see my hillside shanty mate again. I later learned that he had been wounded while guiding a tank among the pillboxes on the island. He was evacuated. He eventually recovered and was assigned to other outfits for the duration of the war. He stayed in the Marine Corps following the war. His widow wrote to me in recent years of his death.

I was in charge of the Headquarters Platoon of the Weapons Company, D Company of First Battalion, Second Marines (D-1-2). This consisted of about thirty-two men, with Gunnery Sgt. Wohlford and Buck Sgt. Clarence Petrie, of Gridley, California. Petrie was the company quartermaster and was in charge of the larger weapons when they were not in use by the several company platoons in training and in combat.

We had rendezvoused in a Higgins boat all day long, just beyond small arms range, in the choppy waters off the little island of Betio, waiting for the word to go onto the beach. The Assistant Weapons Company Commander, Captain "Casey"

Lewis*, was also in our Higgins boat. When word came to go in, we all walked off the Higgins boat ramp at the end of a pier that jutted out into the water about eight hundred feet from the beach. Only Lewis remained in the boat as I led the men along, in and out of the pier pilings, toward the beach.

Struggling forward in the water, every man carried a heavy can of belted .30 caliber machine gun ammunition in each hand and his weapon strapped over his shoulder. I led the single file column with Petrie next and "Gunny" Wohlford at the rear to keep anyone from dropping out of the column. We passed a number of dead marines and Japanese among the pilings along the way. We arrived on the beach without casualty.

As I recall, while I was wading in toward the beach, in and out of the pier, having anticipated the action all day, my waterworks went out of control. It didn't seem to matter since I was in the water anyway. In fact, the whole time that I was on the island before being hit, I went without a single bowel movement. I don't recall seeing a fellow marine take the time to perform such an act. A marine would have been a sitting target had he done so. A Japanese sniper would have received extra points in Japanese Heaven for shooting one of us in such circumstances.

I later found out that First Lt. William Hawkins, Commander of the Second Marines Scout Sniper Platoon of thirty-four men plus a squad (about eight or ten men) of combat engineers had been given the special assignment of clearing out the nests of snipers and Japanese positions located along the pier before our coming ashore. That job involved fighting so fierce that Hawkins had been wounded twice in hand-to-hand encounters. To our great good fortune he did his job well. Our platoon's lack of casualties was the best evidence of this.

By the time we made it to the beach, it was getting dark. Lieutenant Colonel "Jim" Crow of the Second Battalion, Eighth Regiment, was establishing his command post with sandbags and such in a bomb crater. Crow had a reputation as an outspoken and colorful "character." I reported to him, told him who we were and asked where Colonel Kyle was located. He told me Kyle was down to the right of the pier and that Colonel David

*Recent Charleston, West Virginia, newspaper obituary recites that Dr. Charles Pell ("Casey") Lewis, who served as a marine in World War II, has died in Reidsville, North Carolina, as an ear, nose and throat specialist, having gained his medical degree at Duke University following the war.

Shoup had established a Division command post in another bomb crater between Crow's and Kyle's command posts. Otherwise, he said, the beach still belonged to the enemy. He said it would be best for me and my men to dig in for the night around his command post. He added, "I might have to throw you in there tonight," indicating he expected a beach counterattack that first night ashore.

I replied, "Aye, aye, sir," and moved a short distance away and conferred with Petrie and Wohlford. We immediately struck out along the water'e edge to find Colonel Kyle. Some time later, remaining in single file, we found Colonel Kyle in his sandbag C.P. We reported our encounter with well-known Colonel Crow. he laughed and told us to dig in around his (the First Battalion, Second) C.P. for the night.

Petrie and I dug in together. He got some sleep sitting in the hole. It was reassuring to hear him snore. I spent the night praying silently, trying to make deals with God to spare me for a better purpose. All night thunder-claps resounded overhead as the relentless shelling of the central airfield continued from offshore.

At dawn the second day, the first sign of activity among the foxholes around Colonel Kyle's C.P. was the figure of Scout Sniper Platoon Leader Hawkins. With fresh bandages on his arms, legs and head, he was jumping in and out of several enemy pillboxes close by, whether they had been cleared of Japanese before or not. It was obvious he was not going to last very long. He was killed that morning. The captured airfield was named after him and he was awarded the Congressional Medal posthumously.

Lieutenant Col. Presley Rixey of the Tenth Regiment Artillery attached to the First Battalion, was in our headquarters group. He had played bridge with our Battalion Officers in the ward room of the ship enroute to the island destination, while I had spent my spare time alone meditating on the deck, looking out to sea and sky, contemplating the real war looming ahead.

The Eighth Marines were our reinforcements. They had been held in reserve, off shore, all night. With the dawn they started wading toward our section of beach. Rixey had his men set up a .75 mm Howitzer to cover them. A coral reef prevented their Higgins boats from coming the final eight hundred feet to the beach. This last stretch of water was waist deep and in some places deeper. The men who had come ashore the previous day

70

were pinned down in disorganized clusters, primarily along the seawall.

We looked seaward as the Eighth Marines slowly waded toward the beach. They held high their weapons, to keep them out of the salty water. They were laden with gas masks, packs, ammunition belts, grenades and the other usual paraphernalia of war. None of these several hundred brave men turned back, but slowly waded on in the face of devastating enemy fire. Casualties were extremely high. Only a small proportion of them finally staggered onto the beach. Some of them collapsed at the very water's edge. The ocean to our front was dotted with the several hundred bodies of marines held afloat by their gas masks and packs before sinking to the ocean floor. From the beach several enemy pillboxes directed their deadly fire on the incoming Eighth Marines. Colonel Rixey was firing his Howitzer almost point blank into the side of the central, and most prominent, pillbox. This rectangular structure jutted out onto the beach to the water's edge.

Property Sgt. Petrie, Wohlford and I, along with a corporal whose name I have forgotten, found a .50 caliber machine gun and ammunition. We made it to the mouth of the same rectangular pillbox at the water's edge. We started firing that gun into the slit of the pillbox which was still firing on the incoming marines. I also called in a Sherman tank to come alongside our .50 caliber machine gun and and fire its canon at the slit of that most central and most lethal pillbox. (Later, at the Pearl Harbor Hospital, a fresh unnatural hole was found in my eardrum thanks to that tank gun at my side.)

The first waves of the landing forces had come in on amphibious tractors. They were able to override the reef and move inland from the beach and Coconut log seawall. Later waves of the invasion came in Higgins boats and had to disgorge, as we had, at the coral reef.

This central pillbox, at the seawall, had stopped an amphibious tractor. The "Amtrac" was stalled half-way up the sea wall. Around it body parts and limbs of marines were strewn in great profusion. The body of a marine named Casto hung half in and half out of the side of the Amtrac. He was from southern West Virginia and of my old "Dog" Company Platoon. (Another Amtrac was disabled about fifteen feet in front of that most lethal pillbox. Its occupants were trapped in a seawall corner where the

Dog Company first wave Amtrac stalled on the sea wall in front of the most devastating interconnected pillboxes. The bodies and assorted parts of bodies, including limbs and hands, are seen along the seawall at this point and cluttered against both sides of the Amtrac. The picture had to be taken after the island was secured and private Casto's body, draped over the left front side of that Amtrac, had been removed

large pillbox jutted out onto the beach to the water's edge.)

A photograph of this particular Amtrac was later taken and appeared in countless publications. The photograph was taken after poor Casto's body (which had been draped over the side) was removed on the fourth day. Thus, after the island was secured and it was safe to recover bodies of our dead.

The Tarawa invasion was more of a general melee than a battle of any orderly dimension. The units had all become fragmented and were proceeding independently, in small groups. Petrie, Property Sgt. of D Company, had access to the ammo and equipment supply dump at the First Battalion Command Post. Petrie and I, along with the unnamed corporal, and at times D Company Gunnery Sgt. Wohlford, worked on the strong point of Japanese defenses. This pillbox may have killed more marines than any other defensive position on the island. (A map showing the Japanese installations and troop emplacements il-

Amtrac stalled on the seawall taken from another angle in front of the devastating Japanese pillbox strong point. A second Amtrac was put out of action on the beach nearby (party visible in picture), trapping the occupants in a corner of the seawall, resulting in total annihilation of these marines in each Amtrac.

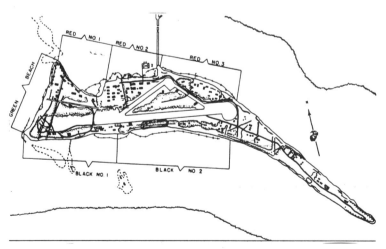

Island diagram of Japanese installations, courtesy of Lt. Col. Joseph H. Alexander, USMCR in naval institute *Proceedings,* November 1993.

73

lustrates why this point was so strong and able to resupply personnel to pillboxes where the two Amtracs were disabled.

We discovered there were a series of connecting, partly underground, trenches between the main pillbox, which had the best view of the ocean approach, and the other pillboxes.

I worked with Petrie and "Gunny" Sergeant Wohlford, fighting intensely in the area of these strong pillboxes. I spent the second day and part of the third day with Petrie, Wohlford and the corporal working back and forth, in and out of these connecting fortifications. We returned often to the ammo supply at Colonel Kyle's C.P., renewing our grenades and TNT charges, including smoke grenades, demolition grenades and other, larger fused TNT charges, as well as conventional hand grenades. We darted and crawled over, around and through these trenches.

On the third day, I was hit. I had gone into the largest, most devastating, central pillbox, the one which had cut the marines to pieces and had stopped the Amtrac on the wall. Inside, I found the bodies of numerous Japanese sprawled on top of each other, some still alive. It was apparent that, as the pillbox had been silenced by our attacks, other Japanese soldiers had crawled in through the partly underground trenches. Crawling over the bodies of their fallen comrades, they would renew firing from the weapons I found strewn about the enclosure.

Inside the pillbox, I found a large Japanese flag with the rays of the sun on it and a very old sword. I still have these souvenirs in my home, preserved with the help of Sergeant Petrie and First Sgt. Edmonds, as hereafter related.

A Japanese sniper had apparently climbed into a wood and tin shack about thirty feet away from us. The shack's sides and roof had mostly been ripped off. I was standing up. My upper torso was visible above the edge of an entrance to the connecting trenches. I turned my head to the right to ask Petrie to toss me more grenades. Then I was hit. The sniper's bullet hit the left side of my neck at the junction of my shoulder. This showed that his aim had been between my eyes just before I had turned my head to the right, away from his angle of fire, to call for more grenades.

Upon being hit, I ducked down in the trench, out of sight. I reflected a quick moment on the fact that my life was not as charmed as my mother had led me to believe. I then quickly jumped out of the hole and was soon back over the seawall. Petrie and Wohlford helped me along the beach to the area of Colonel Kyle's Command Post. Here Petrie found my bridge-playing friend, the mustached battalion, Dr. Smith, who gave me two plasmas there on the beach. Dr. Smith personally hailed a Higgins boat to take me to a ship which was receiving the stream of casualties.

Petrie placed my framed, miniature colored picture of my deceased sister Sarah on my stretcher. My Bible, bound like a law book, given me by my father and inscribed when I was leaving his presence to board the train for the west coast, and the flag and sword from the pillbox, were also placed on my stretcher. All of these items had been retrieved by Petrie from my gear and pack at Colonel Kyle's C.P., near where I was being treated by Dr. Smith. Property Sgt. Petrie was adept at the business of storage and supply.

Apparently, sometime after I had been hit and evacuated, Petrie and "Gunny" Wohlford, both machine gun and mortar ordnance experts, catalogued the enemy weapons within that pillbox emplacement we had worked so hard to silence. They must have reported all this to Colonel Kyle, because the silenced weapons were enumerated in the Navy Cross Citation I was later awarded. (Many wild and harrowing tales about the dimensions of the fighting began circulating on the fourth day, when the island was declared "secured.")

The Higgins boat started for the hospital ship, tossing up and down on the waves, with its load of maimed and dying marines lying against the side wall of the boat. My clothes were mostly cut off of me, and my rank was not very apparent. One man, with no visible wounds, was acting wild and making himself very obnoxious. He just needed some positive therapy. I gave it to him. I told him that if he didn't shut up and sit down I would shoot him. He quieted down.

I remember being hoisted from the Higgins boat in a rope basket sling from the end of a boom. I glided through the air and landed aboard the hospital ship (a converted liberty ship). I landed on a "poop deck" in the midsection of the ship. Here the casualties were receiving first aid from the doctors. A doctor asked me where I was from. He gave me a shot of sodium pentothal, then asked me to sing "Dixie". I got halfway through the first bar, as the doctor cleaned my wound, when my lights went out.

After what seemed like a day or more, with the ship under-

Picture sent to me after the war by Sgt. Clarence Petrie, tough and resourceful, no-nonsense property sergeant, wounded and malaria inflicted in Guadalcanal, who jealously mothered the machine guns and mortars of the battalion when they were not in actual combat or training use. His know-how and access to the supply and ammo dump at the battalion C.P. was the key to our efforts to silence the interconnected pillboxes. I understand he was much later awarded the Navy Cross for his conduct.

way, I awoke below deck. I was lying in a bunk among rows of bunks stacked three or four deep. All around me the sounds of

Picture of my sister, Sarah, and my bible,
which remained with me through the war.

the wounded begging, yelling "corpsman" and "water," a bedlam
of moans and groans, filled the darkened ship's hold. After some
time, a corpsman checked my dog tags and found I was an officer. Accordingly, I was moved topside to a stateroom with three
other officers for the rest of the way to Pearl Harbor.

Often, each day, the ship's loudspeaker announced "quiet
about the ship during the burial of the dead." The dead were

sewed into canvas and slid overboard from a chute, into the briny deep. This was accompanied by the playing of taps by the bugler sounding over the loudspeaker.

The physical hurt and pain from my wound did not compare with the sinking feeling I felt that my life was not as safe as my saintly mother had led me to believe. On more mature reflection, and four months of convalescence in the Aiea Heights Naval Hospital at Pearl Harbor, I began to credit my mother's prayers with keeping the "dum-dum" (explosive) bullet from hitting me between the eyes. Instead, the bullet entered immediately beside the carotid artery at the left base of my neck and exited from a much larger hole several inches down my back. The bullet just missed the main artery and missed penetrating my chest wall, which would have caused me to drown in my own blood. Two years later remaining copper fragments caused sinus track infections and had to be surgically removed at the University Hospital in Charlottesville where I was attending a graduate law course after the war and after being married.

Official reports of the battle recited that the few Japanese prisoners taken were interviewed at the conclusion of the fighting and asked, "Was there any moment when your moral flagged?" Their reply was, "When the dying marine just kept coming." This was an obvious reference to the Eighth Regiment Marines wading into the beach on the second morning.

I heard much later that Colonel Rixey was awarded the Navy Cross for his action. Admiral Nimitz pinned a purple heart on me in a front parking lot formation at the Naval Hospital at Pearl Harbor. He also pinned the Navy Cross on me on the Second Division parade ground on the Parker Ranch on the big island of Hawaii several months later. (Many years later, I heard that Petrie had died of a brain tumor at his home in Gridley, California.)

Shortly before the Tarawa campaign, I had been reassigned to "Dog" Company Headquarters Platoon of miscellaneous personnel. It was my old first platoon, including Private Casto, from West Virginia, who died hanging half in and half out over the side of an Amtrac, that was in the first wave landing on Red Beach Two.

It is simply the inscrutable action of fate, or Kind Providence, in my life that allows me now to write this story instead of being buried in the sands of Betio Island. I was hospitalized for about four months at the beautiful Aiea Heights Naval Hospital overlooking Pearl Harbor. Here gentle night breezes provided me with the best sleep of my life. I was ambulatory most of the time. My wound slowly granulated back in to fill the gaping hole the explosive bullet had plowed through my left shoulder.

Bridge became my passion. I teamed up with an Army Air Force Squadron Commander, whose name I have forgotten. Together we reviewed our bridge hands during the day to sharpen our games in the evening. We became the champs of the officers' top floor ward-room. Our competition was the other officers, both patients and doctors. I was much recovered physically by the time I left the hospital and my bridge game was at the point of perfection. I didn't draw my pay because my bridge winnings kept me well supplied while in the hospital.

"All things worked together" for my good - fate was kind to me in a rough way - an answer to my mother's constant prayers.

My loss of the editorship in college threw me into law school just in time to complete my law course and to go to war. During the period of war preparation and training in New Zealand, I was dealt another blessing in disguise. I was transferred from my original D Company Platoon. This prevented me from being in the ill-fated Amtrac, which carried part of my original platoon to sure death in the first landing wave on Tarawa beach.

Instead of being obliterated on the Tarawa beach, I was shot in the side of my neck. Thus, I survived serious, but not fatal wounds to write this account.

When I was strong enough I rejoined the Second Division, First Battalion. They were retraining at newly-established "Camp Tarawa" in the middle of the famous Parker Ranch on the Big Island of Hawaii. The Parker Ranch was second in size only to the King Ranch in Texas. It was located on a vast plateau below the spectacular, snow-capped peak of Mauna Kea Volcano.

I spent my nights at an adjoining Army Hospital mobile unit, a long wooden tin-roofed hut, in one of two rooms at the end of the building. A central aisle separated bunks on each side of the long room. As fortune would have it, my room and the nurse's room were at the end of this unit and across from each other, one of the war's small vagaries. My wound was still draining and healing and growing back together. The nurse's hometown was Beckley, West Virginia, thirty-five miles from my hometown. Other Princeton hometown boys not in the picture were: (1)

Three hometown boys - Lt. Col. Glen Workman, G-2 (Intelligence officer) 7th Air Force at Hickham Field at Pearl Harbor and, later, on Saipan; Ronald Lee ("Buddy") Russell, Marine Medium Bomber pilot stationed on Saipan (who took me on an unofficial bombing run over nearby small island and who later served 37 distinguished years at home and abroad in CIA scientific activities); and, Sanders C.O. of "A" Company.

Cpl. Robert Thorn, of Second Battalion, Second Regiment, Marines, whose long-term camp on Saipan was immediately below our first battalion camp in the middle of a large cane field, with a sandbag outdoor theater located between our two camps, for our joint use, to see movies - the straggling Japanese holdouts sometimes also watched from the hillside outskirts; and, (2) Sgt. Darrell ("Curly") Whittaker, of the Eighth Marine Regiment, who often came to my "A" Company headquarters with my Sergeant Stickles, signing out on liberty to visit other camps around the island. Both "Curly" Whittaker and Stickles were well over six feet tall and outstanding physically. "Curly's" father, Arthur Whittaker, worked on the Virginian Railway and served as a city policeman in our hometown. Stickles and Whittaker had gone through marine training together and Whittaker now tells me that Stickles had flunked out of officer's school for "knowing more than the instructors." Stickles was lost on patrol around Tapotchau when he bravely stationed himself as a connecting link between small squad patrols searching the jungle for hold-out Japanese. His body was not recovered by our company after several days attempt. It was later discovered by Third Battalion (Second Regiment) patrol in their turn at patrol activities. Japanese holdout Captain Obo's group probably killed Stickles and "A" Company Sgt. Channing Miller, who was taken to the Saipan Hospital before he died. The only two, but very valuable men, "A" Company lost in our year-long patrolling on Saipan - the difference was Channing Miller never lost touch with his squad patrol, whereas, Stickles became isolated in the jungle. Captain Obo knew his terrain better than we did and the only way to eradicate the wiley rascal would have been to station a long-term permanent group to stay on Tapotchau until they outwitted Obo on his own turf. Instead, Obo was able to surrender himself and his squad to the marines in a formal ceremony after the A-Bomb dropped and Japan surrendered.

During the day, I assumed my newly-assigned position as Assistant Commander of A ("Able") Company, officially called "Executive Officer." The commanding officer was Captain Lou Brooks. He was from Greensboro, North Carolina. He had joined the marines prior to the war. As a regular, Brooks was serving with the Second Division in Iceland when the war broke out and when the Second Division joined the First Division on the Solomon Islands in the South Pacific. He was famous in the corps as a champion weight lifter. He had a body like Little Abner of the funny papers, without enough hips to hold his pants up, and shoulders and legs rippling with muscles.

As executive officer, my duties cast me in working relation with Company Gunnery Sgt. Bob Boyd. His six feet three inches tall brother, Paul, was platoon sergeant of the Second Platoon of the same company.

During this time, two men of the company had gone on liberty to the capitol city of the Big Island, Hilo, on the east coast. They got very drunk on synthetic alcohol "island whiskey." They proceeded from Hilo on the long trek up the side of the mountain to the town of Honakau, near the eastern border of the Parker Ranch. At Honakau, in the late evening, they stole a new Packard car from the home of the president of the local bank. They drove off along the narrow paved road which ran through the open, unfenced pastures of the Parker Ranch. These pastures were filled with cactus and coral rock outcroppings.

They drove along traveling off the road as much as on it. As they came near the large marine tent encampment, the Packard played out, much worse for the wear. They abandoned the car and walked the rest of the way, fighting any and everyone along their path, until they were subdued by their tent mates and put to bed in their own cots. The next morning, the Military Police

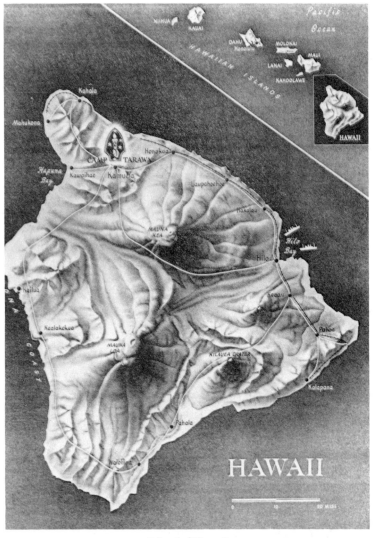

Island of Hawaii.

arrived and hauled the two men to the brig.

As a lawyer and as executive officer, and because I resided at the Mobile Army unit hospital barrack and not with my men, I had the time to take their case. I defended these two men in the general Court Martial trial that followed. The case was tried before a board of officers with the rank of captain and above. Court was convened in a tent.

The trial resulted in acquittal for my clients. The defense was "temporary insanity," resulting from drinking the synthetic Island whiskey. My "expert" witness on the effect of synthetic alcohol was "Gunny" Bob Boyd. Bob had been chief bartender and bouncer in one of the best bars in Indianapolis, run by his widowed mother. He apparently had a reputation around that city as the toughest bouncer in the business. Challengers from all over town were unable to get the best of him.

The day following the trial, Division Commander General Lucian Smith, sent, by runner, a written General Order to all units. It was ordered that thereafter a plea of temporary insanity induced by drinking Island synthetic whiskey would not be permitted in Court Martial proceedings. Military criminal law in the combat theater was changed ipso stanto, with a stroke of the pen of the commander.

The Honakau banker had been a regular guest of General Smith at the general's home. This home, loaned to him by the ranch owner, was located in a grove of trees in the center of the Parker Ranch. Here, the general and the banker often played the ancient and honorable card game known as bridge.

Thus, my reputation was established as executive officer of "Able Company." At last, my law schooling was worth something at war. Later, this incident paid off in practical terms, as the fighting wore on, on the Saipan Island in the Marianas.

Saipan and Tinian Campaigns

Colonel Kyle's First Battalion, as a reward for its conduct at Tarawa, was selected to make a minus H hour D-Day landing on the east coast Magiciene Bay of Saipan. The landing was to be in the nighttime, by rubber boats rowed in noiseless stealth. From the landing, we were to proceed from the beach in single file to the high point (1500 foot), Mt. Tapotchau. There we were to form a perimeter defense around the peak, denying this high

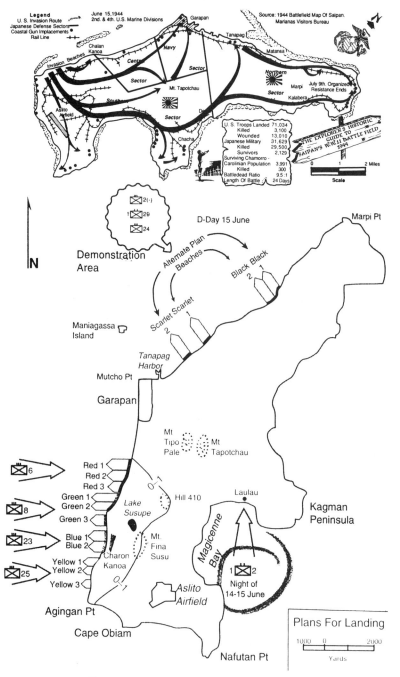

Two maps and battle plans of Saipan Island.

ground to the enemy island defenders.

We trained religiously on the black beaches of Kona on the west coast of Hawaii for months, and were in top physical condition. We were even plied with raw carrots in our diet to sharpen our night vision.

This special mission was called off, however, after the battalion went to sleep on our transport APDs (converted destroyers, each carrying one stripped-down company of 120 men and officers, plus the ship's crew), specially selected for this mission. These small ships had bounced around in the water on our trip from Hawaii to the Marianas producing extensive seasickness among us, especially in "A" Company Platoon Leader Creel. As it turned out, we landed on one of the western regular landing beaches, in the second wave of the invasion.

Creel was an Arkansan. He was hit on the second or third day after we landed, at Flame Three Hill, coming into Garapan town, the Island capitol. The wound was in his stomach area. Weak and undernourished from constant nausea, he died quickly. Creel had stashed away some of his war souvenirs among the rocks of Flame Three Hill's slope. This proved to be a special shrine or worship place (or park) for the Japanese defenders, who gave up this ground very reluctantly.

When our company advanced around Sugar Loaf Mountain and through Flame Tree Hill and to the Sugar King Statue and park (located in the southeast outskirts of Garapan town), we skirmished through the dwellings of Japanese families in the park area. The small, wooden, oriental one-story houses had been knocked to smithereens by our previous bombardment and all of the contents of the houses were littered all over the place, to be destroyed by sun, rain and eventual clean up by the bulldozer. I paused long enough to pick up some photographs from the homes occupied by Japanese military families and put them in my pack. I mailed them home (passed and stamped on the back by the Second Division censor), where my mother put them in an album. I show some of these photographs here to show the super-pride of race, preferring suicide to surrender, with which we were dealing in this war in the Pacific.

While going through the park, the bigger-than-life statue of the Sugar King remained intact except for numerous small-arm bullet holes which the marines inflicted as we passed through. On our fifty year return to the island, the old Sugar King statue

87

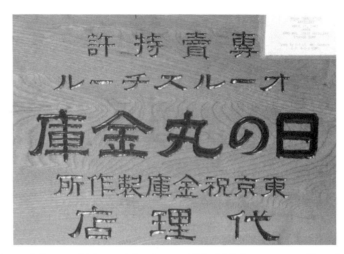

Picture of plaque, which was taken by me off the high fence surrounding a huge Japanese ammunition dump at the edge of the Garapan Town area. The plaque is roughly translated, "Artillery April 21, 1943 - Japan Arms Mfg., etc."

Demolished sugar factory.

still stands.

When we went through Garapan, I removed a wooden sign from the high wire fence around a mammoth Japanese ammunition storage area. This sign hangs above the door to the "head" in my private office at the present time. A day or so after we advanced north of Garapan, we could see in the distance the ammo dump burning and exploding in all directions, having been set afire by our rear eschelon forces.

Sugar King statue.

In the press of this campaign, many of life's basics were abandoned as luxuries. We wore the same dungarees for about twenty-five days and nights straight and had one change of socks in our packs. We washed our hair, bodies and dungarees at the same time, without undressing, by soaping up and standing in the frequent and refreshing rains. Our packs also contained very small rolls of toilet paper. Our rations consisted mostly of "C" ration cans of three varieties; (1) beans, (2) hash and (3) stew. After some monotonous days, reissue would vary our rations with a "K" ration packet of cheese, a beef broth tablet to dissolve in water, crackers and ham or spam, along with another miniature roll of toilet paper.

Each man and officer used the trenching tool attached to his pack, a short handle small spade, to dig a small hole and cover the same in cat fashion after his daily relief. The trenching tool was not as useful digging foxholes at night, as was the outer metal cover of our helmets, which also served as pillows for sleeping. The poncho in our pack covered us from rains during movement or in sleeping.

We moved forward in skirmish-line formation, northward, on an island wide front each day. We dug in each night. How far we moved each day depended on how much opposition we had to take out. The Japanese were disorganized and the marine philosophy was to keep them that way. At night, we took turns staying awake in our two-man holes. The disorganized enemy came into our lines in the night and caused some disruption. They were trained as night fighters and used the night to reorganize and reoccupy some positions and bunkers they had lost during the day. These positions in our rear caused confusion the next day and had to be cleared out again in order to move forward. In the day time, swarms of flies from the decaying dead, both human and animal, competed for our food – we simply picked them out of our food and continued eating. In the night, mosquitoes were ever present. We held them at bay by rubbing repellent on our faces and other exposed areas.

The first night, Bob Boyd and I dug our hole in a grove of trees near the beachhead in sight of the huge, towering tin building which was the Charan Kanoa Sugar Refinery. It was too rocky to dig very deep and we built a parapet of coral rocks around us and partially over us. During the night we came under heavy fire. Several officers and men who had dug in within talking distance of our hole died in this shelling. First Lt. Windham, from North Carolina, and Second Lt. "Big Swede" Andersen, both of whom had joined the battalion just prior to this island campaign, were among those killed close by our foxhole. Bob and I spent the night throwing the persistent sand crabs out of our specially constructed foxhole. Bob's amusement with the crabs was very reassuring to me as a younger person with much less worldly experience than old Bob had under his belt.

When we had advanced about three-fourths of the way toward the north end of the island, a little beyond Tanapag Harbor, the Japanese mounted a large night counterattack. The counterattack centered on the line of the 27th Army Infantry Division and broke through. The counterattack was only stopped by point blank, short fused artillery fire from the tenth Marine Artillery Regiment, which was backing up the 27th Army line.

Our First Battalion was moved from the east side. We came down and around to the area of the southern airfields. Then, in trucks along the east side, we went back up to the front. Here we debarked and went across the island's central ridge above Tanapag. We pinned down a large pocket of Japanese who had penetrated the 27th line. That day we made a quick, lateral advance. We herded them against the beach just over a small, coral, cave-pocketed cliff, near the water's edge, on the west coast. That day Able Company lost by injury every officer, excepting Captain Brooks and me. Approaching the beach, Lieutenant Shelton Goodwin, a valuable officer from Magnolia, Arkansas, got a shell fragment in his leg and had to be hauled off. Coming down the slope of the central island ridge toward the beach earlier in the day, newly-assigned Lieutenant Stanfield, a spit and polish parade ground officer with a neatly-trimmed mustache, was standing beside me at the face of a rock cliff when an enemy bullet struck the rock face and sent small fragments of rock into the side of Stanfield's jaw and neck, causing superficial flecks of blood to appear on his skin. He elected to go back to sick bay. That was the last I saw of him. Late in the day, Brooks went over the small cliff to the beach to see the situation for himself. A grenade exploded in front of him, peppering his giant torso. I went over and directed the men to carry him off on a stretcher. Once on the stretcher, Brooks shouted out loud and clear, "Sandy, take over!". Thus, I became the company commander and the only officer left in the company for the eventful night that was to follow.

We set up rolls of barbed wire on our company's front, paralleling the short beach and small cliff. We dug in our holes for the night attack that was sure to come. We sighted in our fields of fire. We placed a heavy, water cooled, .30 caliber machine gun on each end of our company's front. Two other machine guns were equally spaced between them. Lesser firepower was stationed between these major points for the expected attack. At the south end of our line, the cliff played out onto level ground, between the small beach and the shore.

An army unit was loosely tied into our southern company front, without any direct communication between us. Communication went back up to battalion and to division and back down the line to the Army Central Command Headquarters. Our best communication was to stay out of each other's way.

At day's end, my company radio man (a Navajo Indian) was hit right through the radio strapped on his back. We were sent a replacement radio man and radio to keep in communication with the battalion during the night. The Japanese understood our English, but not the language of the Navajo. These stoic radio communicators were all called by the rest of us, "Chief." They certainly deserved the title because of their valuable service.

Colonel Kyle offered to send a certain replacement officer. None of the other companies had wanted this officer. I refused. Even without trouble brewing, I didn't want him. We had a good team. First Sgt. Johnny Dean, from the Arkansas Ozarks, and the two Boyd brothers were my main assurance that the line would hold.

During the night the attack came and lasted until dawn. The cornered Japanese mounted a desperate assault. The fighting was so intense that we ran very low on machine gun ammunition during the night. Colonel Kyle sent more ammunition down from the slope command post by jeep, driven by single driver, Corporal Jackson (a former member of my "Dog" Company platoon.) Jackson unloaded fast and hightailed it back up to the mountainside battalion C.P. During the night, the left (southern) flank machine gun was knocked out. The right (northern) flank was not then receiving much action. Gunny Bob Boyd carried the heavy, right flank machine gun, fully assembled, tripod and all, on his shoulders, the entire length of the company line, to replace the disabled gun.

93

The line held. At daybreak, Colonel Kyle radioed saying that regiment wanted to know what all the fuss in our line was about. He asked for a head count of enemy dead on our front, as well as our own casualties. I sent Platoon Sergeant Paul Boyd and Gunnery Sergeant Moore under our wire to make the count of the enemy. After a while, they returned to my sandbag C.P. at the middle rear of our line. Moore still had a cigarette dangling from his lips and was grinning. His first words were, "I got my ticket stateside!" Then, he gave me the Japanese head count of 350 Japanese dead. This included the one who rose up and shot him through the buttocks.

Our own casualties were twenty-seven dead or wounded. This included several hit on the day's advance to the beach cliff top position.

I went to the left flank to see the pile up of dead Japanese. At the water's edge and the cliff's end lay those who had tried to come around our line at this point. The beach and the water were littered with Japanese on top of each other. The waves of the water lapping on the beach were red for a distance of thirty feet out from the shore.

Corporal Hinajosa and Squad Leader Sergeant Sizemore from West Virginia, who had been wounded on Tarawa was with me in the little Army Mobile Hospital Unit shack. Before we left Hawaii and shoved off for the Marianas Campaign, Sizemore and I had the option of going back stateside for reassignment or remaining with our outfit. Both of us chose to remain with our outfits, rather than to be reassigned in the states to other units. Hinajosa was killed that afternoon and Sizemore that night.

Gunnery Sergeant Bob Boyd was issued the Silver Star award and I received a Bronze Star Citation for the night's fire fight. Bob had told me he was shot on Guadalcanal through the crease of his chin and lower lip and out his back. He was carried through the jungle by litter and dropped so often he got up and walked to a jeep ambulance, which also shuffled him so much that he got out and walked back to the aid station for treatment. Later in life, he died of bone cancer (of his jaw bone.) We kept in close touch until his death. I went out to visit him a time or two after the war.

Saipan was officially declared "secured," even though there were several thousand Japanese still running around loose all over the island and, especially among the jungle slopes and caves of Tapotchau. We were given a few days' rest and a change of clothes. We had a little party at my sandbag C.P. foxhole, rigged up with shelter halves as a tent roof. The company officers and sergeants were enjoying some "saki." Colonel Kyle had sent over from his nearby hilltop C.P. some beer sent to him by a ship captain friend anchored off the coast. We were called down by Colonel Kyle via the sound power phone when we got too loud. The Japanese were still lurking around the area.

A letter I wrote home in this interlude between Saipan and Tinian was copied by my father's secretary and preserved by my mother in her scrapbook.

July 15, 1944

Dear Mother, Daddy and Caroline:

At long, long last, I have a moment I can write a letter to let you know that I survived the whole vicious campaign of Saipan. Last night was the first time since landing here a month ago that I have been able to sleep with my shoes off and, day before yesterday is the first day that I was able to change from the clothes in which I landed. They were more like armor than clothes, they were so stiff with filth. It's been beyond imagination, but I'm so grateful to have come through unscathed and my most serious ailments have been two cases of dysentery and cat fever (102 degree temperature) for two days. I didn't miss a minute of the show and found that a man can keep going as long as he's conscious, and that sometimes he doesn't know conscious, he's so numb. Our outfit is composed of wonderful men built into the strongest of timber by the tempering process of the Marine Corps, administered the old fashioned way from the Second Division. There's never a complaint and every man knows that all he has is the only limit of what is expected of him; while the Army and other outfits get some conveniences, we don't expect them, and every private takes pride in his knowledge that we are much superior in our job for being without them.

Every officer in the Company was injured except me, although three of them are now back with us. I am now Company Commander and my responsibility

*has lept considerably. I can't begin to express how
proud I am to command such a magnificent company.*

*Darkness and mosquitoes force me to close this
for now. I understand tomorrow is Sunday - the first
week day I've recognized since June 15. P.S. July 16*

*I just got back from church and will finish this
letter and get it off today. Everyone at church had his
rifle and had his helmet at his side or sitting on it
and a small mopping up skirmish was going on within
100 yards and, thus, our singing was punctuated.*

*I must go to chow now. We built a Company gal-
ley yesterday and no longer open our own cans of rations, but eat all together. Will write again soon.*

Love and devotion,
William

Tinian

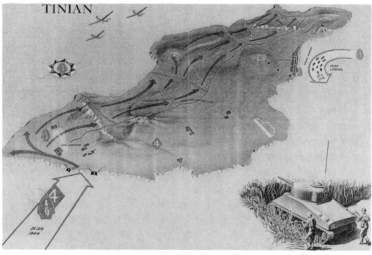

Tinian Island battle plan map, showing Second Division going down the left
(east) half of the island, with the Fourth Division on the west half of the island.
Our company was the extreme left (eastern) side of advancing skirmish line and
we halted on the coastline looking across at the Japanese suicide rites.

After the short rest interlude on Saipan, we boarded LST's
(Landing Ship's Tank) for Tinian, an island two miles from
Saipan. We walked off the front ramp of those ships directly

onto small, improvised, rough landing docks at the island's northwest coast. We crossed the airfield, which our forces later converted to B-29 strips to bomb Japan and from which the Enola Gay B-29 was launched to drop the A-bomb on Japan.

A two Division (Second and Fourth Marines) skirmish line moved abreast down to the south end of the island in eight days. It was the perfect campaign you almost never hear about. I, however, had dengue fever the first few days and was dragged along by First Sergeant Johnny Dean. I did not want to turn in to sick bay for fear of losing my new command of the company. I had picked up a little Japanese canvas aluminum folding stool when crossing the airport. Every time we stopped, I would sit on the stool and rest, with a high fever. One night, after crossing the airport, Johnny and I woke up locked in a wrestling match between us, each thinking we had a Japanese in our C.P. dugout. It might have simply been my dengue delirium, and we ended the bout by fanning the pungent odor of our armpits in each other's faces and laughing deliriously before going on back to sleep.

The two division line pivoted on the right with the Fourth Division's western beach front. "A" Company First Battalion Second Division became the extreme left (eastern) flank, along the rugged eastern coastline. We had the impossible job, which takes a little longer, of going through the roughest jungle and coral rock terrain. We had to keep abreast of the entire two division front, in swing-tail fashion as on the playgrounds of our younger days. We had no choice but to advance in squad single files through the jungle trails. Our task was complicated by the fact that most of the islanders, along with the Japanese, indistinguishably disguised as civilians, were hiding-out in the rocky jungles to our front. Therefore, we took many more prisoners than the other outfits. They had all congregated in the boondocks in our area of advance.

Johnny Dean kept an elderly Japanese man for several days to carry his pack and to bow and scrape to everyone along Johnny's way, until I decided to send the man back to headquarters. The man had excellent manners and Johnny delighted in having such a first-class aide to carry his gear. Battalion Intelligence Officer Lieutenant "Dutch" Shultz soon radioed me that the fellow was a Japanese general and was, in fact, the quartermaster for the Japanese forces on Tinian Island.

Lieutenant Herber, from Chicago, a railway engineer on the Sante Fe Chief, and Lieutenant Goodwin, from Magnolia, Arkansas, had returned to the company. We had a good replacement Platoon Leader in a young Baptist preacher from Texas named Pearson, who joined the Marine Corps after his best friend, marine, had been killed on Guadalcanal. We had a good working team running the company and making a steady and orderly advance down the east coast of the island. Our eighth day advance was ordered to halt just prior to reaching the high cliff on the southern tip of the island. We were to await army replacements.

During these few days of halting and waiting in a very dry season, we observed the Japanese going through suicidal rites off the southeastern high cliffs and onto the rocky beaches below, just as they had done on the north high cliff point of Saipan earlier. I recall thinking that the extremely dry season and lack of water must have contributed to their hopeless state of mind, still unable to understand a religion that authorized suicide, above surrender.

While halted at this point, Johnny Dean, on patrol, captured a Japanese. He took him into a large cave and tried to persuade others to come out. The others declined the invitation and turned on the Japanese soldier. Johnny was able to retrieve the soldier, cut, battered and bruised, and bring him back to my C.P., where he was safely treated and made a Prisoner of War. We let him know that his action was appreciated and gave him first-class medical treatment. He had done his best to persuade the large group of Japanese families to come out of the cave and surrender.

After the battle to take Tinian, Johnny Dean and the Boyd brothers were reassigned, along with all the other Guadalcanal veterans, back to the states. Johnny was later reassigned to the newly-formed Fifth Division. He lost an eye on Okinawa. Later he married his nurse in a navy hospital in California. A few years later, without prior announcement, he suddenly appeared with his wife and three sons, pulling an open canvas covered trailer of furniture, at my law office in southern West Virginia. He had graduated from Stanford University Law School under the G.I. Bill. He remained to practice with my father and me for a year or so, but those were tough times financially, with my father suffering from a brain tumor, and he and his wife felt the need to move back to California in search of more opportunity and where she could work in a larger hospital. He has maintained a solo criminal practice ever since and has become a part-time judge in his semi-retirement. As this book goes to print, I received a letter from Johnny, divorced from his second wife, telling me he was retiring and coming back to his native home in the Arkansas Ozarks.

"A" Company Platoon Sergeant Bill Rogal and his Platoon Leader Bill Herber, whom he had rescued from entrapment on Saipan with the aid of a Sherman tank; both had been hit in the area of the Sugar Loaf Mountain near Garapan Town, halfway up the east coast of Saipan. After the war, Rogal also studied law and became an outstanding anti-trust lawyer, with offices on Connecticut Avenue in Washington, near the capitol. He was also the personal attorney representing famous Tarawa war correspondent and author, Robert Sherrod, and he prepared Sherrod's Last Will and Testament before his recent death. Rogal and his wife Pearl, have exchanged several visits with us and he invested and lost $25,000 in my failed hotel enterprise. Both Bill Rogal and Paul Boyd keep in close touch with me and have visited us several times.

At this writing, Rogal is Judge Advocate and Paul Boyd is Sergeant at Arms of the Second Marine Division Association, which holds annual, week-long conventions at different locations. At a convention several years ago, several of us First Battalion men and wives were seated at a large round table in the banquet hall of the convention center. The banquet, which concluded the activities of several days, was in its final midnight exuberance. A group of large and burly Italian Marines at a nearby table were milling around their table loudly singing opera. Paul left our table, saying, "We can't have this." He went over in the midst of the Italian crowd and said, "Let's sing country western." Tension was ripe for a few minutes but, soon, the Italians joined Paul in country western and around the floor the groups swung and swayed, bellowing country western.

Paul was a very tall and angular man. His platoon leaders were shot on each of three island operations and Paul took over the platoon without a lieutenant for the greater part of these battles, including Guadalcanal, Tarawa and Saipan (Lieutenant Creel was killed the third day at Saipan.)

I vividly remember Paul singing his favorite song on the

high ground stopping point near the southern tip of Tinian. We were camped for several days out in the open, with great views over the sea to the east and south, just like a bunch of boy scouts, without a care and simply waiting for word to be picked up by trucks to take us off the island. We were making our individual fires and concocting whatever kind of food we could scrape up from the Japanese storage caves or elsewhere. Paul did a lot of open-air singing on the scenic ocean overlook, his favorite being "On Top of Old Smokey," a leading country western song of the time.

While we were, thus, waiting, the Japanese were in our full view across the valley, with their families jumping off of the high cliff to their deaths of the rocky southeast shoreline below. We watched this gruesome show, in detail, with a pair of field glasses that we somehow acquired. We were powerless to stop the show.

Lately Johnny Dean and I have corresponded and he explains the incident of his capture of the Japanese Quartermaster General as well as the later incident at the end of the Island of Tinian where he captured a Japanese soldier and used him to try to persuade other Japanese to surrender. His words explaining the details of these two incidents are as follows:

First, the Japanese General: "As we proceeded on Tinian I was out front doing something stupid, I suppose, when the voice said, 'Ma-reen, Ma-reen!' I invited him from the buses. When he came I gave him a cigarette and he said 'Ah, Camel.'

"He was dressed in civilian clothes and as I questioned him said he worked for, I believe, a sugar company. He never supported the war, etc.

"After our friendly chat, I thought how nice the British once had it with their aides, so, I invited him to carry my pack. He even dug a foxhole for me.

"You know, I had that sucker about three days.

About the second incident at the end of the advance at the southern end of Tinian when Johnny captured a Japanese soldier and used him to try to persuade other Japanese to surrender and quit their suicide off the cliffs Johnny explains as follows:

"The facts are, we had three Japanese prisoners. As you recall people were jumping in the ocean. Down the side of the cliff about twenty or thirty feet was a ledge about ten feet wide. I directed one of the prisoners to go down hoping we could save the civilians. The kid did not want to climb down the rocks. With my Carbine pointing to the ledge and back to his head he got the message. As soon as he came down to the bottom of the cliff,

Sanders on Saipan and at chicken compound.

with me at his side, here came the officers waiving their swords. The officers made no attempt to hit me but whacked him on the head and cut off a couple of fingers plus other cuts.

"After I shot the officers, I put the Little Jap on my back and came back up the cliff.

"I'll never forget I sent the Japs with Appleby back to Battalion. I announced to the Japs, that if they understood English, Private Appleby was a conscientious objector and he would not shoot anyone. However, Appleby came back safely."

Note: Appleby was our company runner on Tinian and after Tinian Appleby and Dean and all the original Guadacanal men were sent back to the states for reassignment. Later after we returned to Saipan my company runner was Neiloboski who is mentioned further in the story.

The Name of the Game – "Command"

The role of the company "runner" leads me to tell the reader something about organization. Each separate company – in our First Battalion of Second Regiment – was allotted one "runner," who was something of a spare part flunky, used primarily to run messages from Company Headquarters, which when not moving and overnight, was the C.P. or Command Post and usually dug in with sandbags and such. The three "Rifle Platoons" (small arms), headquarters personnel (captain and his executive officer and first sergeant, company gunnery sergeant, and other administrative personnel), kept communication and direction of the Rifle Platoons of thirty-two men each, with their lieutenant, platoon leader, and his platoon sergeant and then squad leaders (buck sergeants or corporals). And when in the field advancing against the enemy, the weapons company of the battalion, with their platoons of heavier weapons, machine guns and mortars, were attached to the three rifle companies, one platoon to each rifle company of the battalion. All these made up a skirmish line, joined laterally to other battalions and then other regiments of several battalions, forming the division.

On Tinian, we had two marine divisions, the Fourth and the Second, drawn out on a single skirmish line of advance, stretched from one side of the island to the other. This network of command of these units, coordinated the advance down the entire island in eight days. On Saipan, it was two marine divisions and an army division (U.S. twenty-seventh) in the middle, advancing abreast up (northward) the larger island.

Command Headquarters of all units backed up this front line all the way along and communication went from the commander of these combined forces to higher headquarters offshore in ships of the landing force armada.

That's briefly and sketchily the way the war is fought and success all depends on effective communication and command between the units.

I think we did a good job on both islands, from company runner on back up to the landing force headquarters and on back to the White House, U.S.A., itself.

Return to Saipan – Patrolling for Japanese Holdouts

We returned to Saipan without the original Guadalcanal officers and men. Colonel Kyle, Johnny Dean and the Boyd brothers had all returned stateside. This made me, a first lieutenant, the senior officer of the entire First Battalion for a short time, with the exception of a replacement battalion commander, Lieutenant Colonel Totman, who had just come from the stateside training schools. New Regimental commander was Full Colonel Cutts, whose father had invented the "Cutts Compensator," a silencer which attached to the end of a firearm. Division Commander, much-respected General Julian Smith, was replaced by General Thomas Watson, famous for his victory at Eniwetok Island and for not allowing his division staff officers to smoke.

Cutts and Totman proved to be bosom buddies. Most weekends found them "in their cups" at Totman's tent or in our officers' mess, a screened-in wooden building, drinking spirits and devouring my eggs. These eggs had been laid by about one hundred chickens which my runner, Nieloboski, and I had collected from all over the island. We caught these chickens roosting at night in trees after their chicken houses (and all other buildings and enclosures) had been destroyed by our shot and shell. We used flashlights to blind the chickens in their tree roosts and put them in gunnysacks for the trip back to camp. We built a large enclosure and fed them on rice that had been stored in the various caves by the Japanese.

Our large chicken compound was near the officers' mess, located on the east hillside. The hillside overlooked the B-29 airstrip in the distance. Nearby was a multi-hole officer's privy, which afforded a grandstand screened view from crapper seats to watch the B-29s come and go on their daily bombing runs to Japan. From these seats we saw a number of failures to either get planes into the air or to make it back to the runway because of some damage inflicted in a raid on Japan or from running out of fuel. Many planes fell into the ocean just off the runways.

"Neil" and I, with Totman sometimes joining us, took many excursions in jeep and trailer and shot many a cow and hog, like the chickens, running loose over the island. Neil slit their throats and bled them on the spot and we took them to the battalion galley (mess). That was a great improvement on Australian Jack-rabbit. Our battalion and officer's mess became the envy of the other unit camps throughout the island. Neil and another company runner, Appleby, in my headquarters, were most resourceful. Neil carried in his pack a long roll of salami, which he sometimes shared with several of us as a real treat and relief from the usual "C" ration fare, as our skirmish line advanced.

Day by day, we advanced in the heat and sweat of the island. At dark, the first sergeant, the gunnery sergeant and I were busy inspecting the line of troops. We sighted in the guns in case of nighttime counterattacks. Meanwhile, Appleby became handy at scrounging up miscellaneous bedding and tin roofing for our headquarters/C.P. He led a charmed life, running across open ground, zig-zagging like a rabbit, carrying messages to other unit commanders.

Communication was the key to the success of any campaign. Runners filled in the gaps of radio by stringing miles and miles of insulated phone line. Wire was strung on the ground along the side of the roads and trails, tying in all units with sound power telephone. Connections were made between platoon to company and battalion to regiment to division and even between companies directly in our steady advance; all as we pushed the enemy before us. The Japanese were ingenious at infiltration and cutting these lines. This required constant patching of the cut lines. The communication engineers and, especially the men carrying the spools of lightweight wire, were real unsung heroes, exposing themselves to enemy fire as prime targets all the way along the advance.

Totman and Cutts were eager to chase the large number of Japanese holdouts around the jungled slopes of Tapotchau. I was often called to Totman's tent by runner to help plot on the maps various pushes, patrols, ambushes, etc. This often occurred at night when they were deep in their cups and high in spirit, after I had hit the sack. For a short time after Totman's arrival, I was upped to Battalion Operations (Bn.3) position, until a higher ranking replacement major arrived. Then I went back to "A" Company command. I was still called into these planning sessions because of my familiarity with the terrain and Japanese holdout places. I got to be something of a privileged character because of my knowledge of the nooks and crannies of jungles and caves running around the slopes of Tapotchau.

The three rifle battalions of the Second Regiment would take turns camping around Tapotchau for a week at a time and keeping score of the Japanese killed. The numerous flies and hot sun reduced them to mere bones in a few days. War is hell and it became a problem to keep some of the marines from collecting bleached-out enemy skulls and even trying to mail them home. The holdouts never surrendered and never got the word that the Imperial Forces were not going to rescue them. In fact, we found out they had been told the marines would torture them, rape their women and murder their children.

After we had been on the island for some time we discovered a long valley trail. It ran through the jungle and connected the island's interior with the bay. Had we known of it earlier we might have carried out our initial nightime rubber boat landing plans. That trail would figure in another operation.

It was my fanciest bit of patrolling. I managed a connected series of ambushes at clearings along this canyon trail. The trail started at the Tapotchau slopes and ran down to Magiciene Bay. At a point near the bay, a huge cave went deep into the mountainside. Besides serving as a home to a horde of bats, the cave contained a vast amount of enemy stores. These stores included numerous sacks of rice and every kind of food stuffs, canned, dried and otherwise. Among the foodstuffs were canned whale meat, squid and other exotic oriental foods.

This was a complicated multiple ambush. We set up in the day time. The clearings were covered and sighted in, including a larger clearing near the mouth of the cave. As nighttime came on, our riflemen were in place, all set to fire at the same time when I gave the signal. I had established my command post in view of the cave's entrance. Wires connecting sound power phones were laid to each clearing from my C.P.

A new replacement, Second Lieutenant Spessard Holland, son of a U.S. Senator from either South Carolina or Florida, was in charge of one of the ambushes. It took a lot of restraining on the phone with him to keep from springing the trap prematurely. We had to whisper on the phones to keep from alerting the prey.

With the nighttime came movement. We silently allowed a large number of the enemy into the cave. We waited in the darkness for them to come back out. We waited for them to return up the canyon with their loads, stopping in groups to rest in each clearing. We waited until we got the maximum number in all clearings. Then I gave the signal to open fire.

The next morning, an inventory of the dead was taken. Totman was ecstatic at the count. However, most of us felt sick. We were shocked to see very many women, some with infants strapped onto their backs or fronts, among the dead.

In both the Saipan and Tinian battles we moved forward each day and dug foxholes each night. Except for the Japanese General, and the fellow dean captured at the conclusion of the Tinian fighting, we took no uniformed prisoners. Another exception was during the third or fourth day on Tinain when three Japanese soldiers stripped down to their waists, raised a white flag on a stick, and rose up out of the tall grass in front of our company line. No one fired on them, but we motioned them into our line and had them escorted to the rear as prisoners. Otherwise, we were up against an enemy who felt it was kill or be killed.

No Japanese would come out of their holes, pillboxes or bunkers, regardless of our urgings and guarantees of safety. We would speak to them in their language in memorized phrases, or by reciting from a small booklet we carried in our dungaree pockets for reference. Still they would not come out. When it was clear they would not surrender, we would throw in a grenade. Invariably, they would then set off their own grenades and kill themselves. Death before surrender. This grim scenario was repeated in the many bunkers and bomb shelter dugouts in our zone.

They would include their families in group suicides. Near the end of our advance on Saipan, we came to a small cluster of rocks and bushes in an otherwise open area. Here we found an apparent family of six or eight adults and children dead and dying from their own hand grenades. A man lay in this cluster of bodies, his face completely obliterated. He was feeling around for another grenade. Some were still alive in this rocky nest of people. This man without a face had to be prevented from finishing the wholesale suicide of his family, and from killing some of us standing by. We shot him before he could finish the job.

I believe, had the atomic bomb not been dropped, the entire Japanese nation would have committed mass suicide on their home island beaches, taking untold numbers of American soldiers and marines with them.

Okinawha and Homeward

Our more than one year sojourn on Saipan, after Tinian, was broken by a trip to Okinawha. There we joined the invasion forces. Our units made a "dummy" landing on the southern beaches on D-day. This was to distract the enemy from the main landing occurring at the mid-western shore. Our ship armada got in battle array. We went over the sides of the ships into the landing boats. We lined up in waves and proceeded toward the beaches. However, when we got fairly close we turned around then returned to the ships. From there we moved up to the main landing area as reserves.

While standing by, in reserve, we became targets for the suicide kamikaze pilots. One hit the ship to our rear. Another hit a ship to the side of our ship. Luckily, wild and frantic air bursts and streaks of shot and shell into the sky blasted most of them into the water before they could hit the ships of our armada.

We stayed there, in reserve, for a period of days. We watched the intense bombardment of the island. We listened to the radio communications back and forth as the battle raged on land. Then, most of our division returned to Saipan. All except the Sixth Regiment and Eighth Regiments. These regiments went ashore to relieve some of the Fourth Marines who had taken the north half of the island. They took over the advance through the capitol city of Naha. They then had to advance through the southern end of the island, upon the failure of the Twenty-Seventh Army to jump off according to general orders. The army was to have advanced after the preparation shelling and bombing, but failed to move day after day.

We returned to Saipan. There we continued patrolling the island in search of enemy hold-outs. We began to prepare for the invasion of the home island. The invasion of Japan itself.

On patrol one day, with a small party, on the lower benches of Tapotchau, we encountered and entered a small shack at the edge of the jungle. This small house was still standing in good shape, in spite of the war. Saipan shanties did not have window glass, due to the tropical climate. It was obvious someone was using the house. We found fresh-pulled green garden onions lying on the shelf at the window. They had been cut and cleaned and couldn't have been out of the ground but a few minutes and were ready to be eaten when we interrupted the occupant. I admired the neat arrangements the occupant had made for survival.

As we were in the house observing the obvious signs of human habitation, I very strongly sensed that the occupant was peering at us a short distance away in the heavy jungle brush. He could have shot one of us between the eyes. However, the rest of us would have promptly blasted him to high Japanese heaven.

Close by the shanty, after a brief search, I found a small, secluded garden in a jungle clearing. Ripening pineapples were chief among its attractive features. I kept the location of this garden a secret. I paid it a number of visits over a period of time, accompanied by faithful Neiloboski, harvesting the delicious pineapples. We donated some of them to our officers' mess and personally delivered some to the patients who were in the greatest misery in our small hospital.

A typed copy of a letter I wrote home at this time was preserved by my mother. It was written after Okinawha and prior to my expected landing on the Japanese home island. In it I prayed to the Creator of all mankind, and not just my own race or creed. The letter shows I was still trying to make a deal with God to preserve me for more useful undertakings than war.

February 16, 1945

Dear Mother, Daddy and Caroline:

Just a short note before I go to bed. Have written once today. A while ago, I read over Daddy's poem he sent on "Memory," by Cowein. It isn't quite the scene that in melancholy moments tugs at my heart but the same tugging is there. My scene is our little house at the top of the hill, the garden, dog pen, slanted apple tree and all. The poem catches at, which is the best anyone can do, the spirit we feel. It is fine.

The other day after supper I walked a good ways to the coast to a spot on the seaward side of a thick row of pines with not another soul anywhere near or in sight or hearing and sat down comfortable on the pine needles within a few yards of a rugged cliff that dropped 150 feet to the lashing sea which ran like that a long distance in both directions. I sat there for at least an hour and a half while sunset changed to dusk. With the sight and sound and smell and feeling of the water, the cliff, and the beautiful awesome expanse of sea, I thought a prayer. I tried to remember it and wrote it down when I came away and back to my tent. Here's the condensed thought and prayer:

Creator and Perpetuator Bless and continue to care for me through many dangers and hard ways as I increasingly need thy help, guidance and mercy.

Bless and continue to preserve in good ways and health my family of father, mother and sister, as they so thoroughly entrust themselves to you.

Keep us all that we may be brought together again and that we may carry on living in a nobler, finer aspect, if it by thy Holy will to do so. And let me find myself and apply myself and amount to something that bespeaks the rendering of a worthy service to society.

Gather together with you my forebears, my untimely departed sister and my departed friends. From your Island among the stars, you with them, look down and have mercy, pity and sustaining love for us awkwardly striving creatures and hasten the day when love and understanding shall be the only ruling force and we shall live in happiness forever.

Goodnight Mother, goodnight Daddy and night night, Caroline!

Love and devotion,
William

Picture in uniform with chest ribbons denoting battles and decorations.

The letter shows that I was praying to the Creator of all races of mankind and was still trying to make a deal with God to spare me for better things.

My thirty-second month in the Pacific, one day I led a small Tapotchau patrol. That day, for the first and last time, I carried a pistol (.45 colt) instead of the usual Carbine. As I came near the top of a hill, I caught the smell of the enemy. Their habit was to foul up a camp, then move on to a new one. At that same moment, a standing uniformed Japanese soldier saw me. He started screaming and running around like a chicken with his head cut off. The rest of the bunch, about fifteen or twenty men in uniform, jumped up from their naps. They disappeared like a covey of quail into the brush. I emptied my pistol after them but hit nothing. I hadn't had time to call up heavier fire power from the other members of the patrol.

That group of uniformed soldiers was probably the famous Captain Obo's band. Captain Obo and his men were especially evasive. They were later honored with a special ceremony of surrender, after the war was over. I am sure Obo has become a Japanese national legend, just like our Southern Colonel Mosby of the War Between the States.

Soon after my embarrassing incident with this slippery band of Japanese holdouts, I departed for home. I was on a ship a few days out of Pearl Harbor when I heard newscaster Henry Kaltenborn's voice come over the ship's loudspeaker, announcing, "The war is over, the war is over."

I came on home after a few days in Pearl Harbor. What followed was an all-night party of five officers and five girls at the Sir Francis Drake Hotel in San Francisco. We picked up the girls from an upper story window of our Sir Francis Drake Hotel room. Our meal for the five couples in the subterranean "Persian Room" club of the hotel was $100.00 for fried chicken, an unbelievable sum of money. While the girls repaired to the powder room, we decided not to tip the "draft dodger waiters" who had served our meal because they had acted so smug and superior to us. (We were dressed merely in our khaki shirts and trousers. Our officer's uniforms had not caught up with us.) The all-male waiters grouped in a corner to decide what to do as we walked out. We were ready for action if they chose to start it. I recall we were drinking "Southern Comfort" that night. Beyond that I have no recollection of the rest of the night. I woke up the next morning across town, in the apartment of one of the girls.

I spent a month or so as a member of the Guard Battalion at 23rd and Constitution Avenue near the Lincoln Memorial in Washington, DC. The secret mission of the battalion was to police a certain section of the district in the case of a race riot. This was, apparently, considered a real potential. However, while I was there our main function seemed to be putting on a first-class wedding for the daughter of Commanding Officer Charlie Dunbeck at one of the Washington clubs. Colonel Dunbeck was a grand old man of World War I vintage. He had a couple of Navy Crosses to his credit. We staged one of the fanciest weddings ever. The Junior and Senior Marine and Navy officers were at their finest.

I was discharged from active service from Colonel Dunbeck's command. I had no idea about a disability pension and, in fact, did not feel disabled in any way. I was my usual rash self. Colonel Dunbeck insisted I should have a physical to determine that I had a disability in turning my head because of the wound and scar tissue in my neck and shoulder.

Picture taken by photographer of the five officers and girls, signed by each one as follows, *left to right*, Barbara Cunningham, Charles Carter, Jeannie Lau, Raymond Marion, Jeannie Harless, Dick Remington, Bill Sanders, Marilyn Shaffer, Jeff Storey and Katherine Shields. Dick Remington and I were members of the same officers class (13th) at Quantico. Charles Carter was a graduate of VPI, not far from my hometown and lived in Farmville, Virginia.

MARRIAGE
AND
MILITARY
GOVERNMENT

Post War Military Government in Germany

And, so was closed my life as a soldier. Once again I undertook my uncertain civilian life. A life that had been interrupted by the nearly four years hiatus of war.

I mustered out of the Marine Corps and returned to Charlottesville and the university. There I signed up for a graduate law course especially arranged for me by my old law professor, Colonel Hardy Dillard and Dean Ribble.

During the war, Colonel Dillard, who was a West Point graduate, had served as director of studies for both the School of Military Government at Virginia and the War College in Washington. He was also a member of the Special Commission of General Wedemeyer that toured Manchuria just after the war to study the Japanese/Chinese war and the atrocities that had occurred there.

With the close of the war chapter of my life I determined to go into government service. I wanted to help patch up the broken world. I showed Colonel Dillard and Law School Dean Ribble my wartime writings. My father had his secretary type them up when I came home from the service. I had titled them "Ruminations Between Battles." Colonel Dillard told me it was too flowery. He gave me a book on English prose by Quillar-Couch, to teach me to make my expressions simpler. That book said it was great to have brilliant flights of words, but then, "kill your darlings."

A graduate law course was devised, whereby I might qualify for a graduate degree in "International Law and Relations." Colonel Dillard served as my principal teacher and mentor. He prescribed readings. I had seminars with Dillard and other professors from law and other graduate schools. One of the seminars was "Comparative Government," taught by eminent Rhodes Scholar, Dr. Robert Gooch. I loved the course but squarely disagreed with him on the virtue of the monarchial system of government.

Colonel Dillard became the dean of the law school for a few years, succeeding Dean Ribble. Later he became president of the World Court sitting at the Hague, Geneva, Switzerland. He died in Charlottesville about 1982.

115

Colonel Dillard, president of the World Court, who set up the Master of International Law program at University of Virginia.

With the war's end in late 1945, and my enrollment in the graduate study course of International Law & Relations, I found myself back in the middle of university life.

I had a good buddy in law school named Tom Mason. He was from Lynchburg, Virginia, and, like me, was a law graduate back from the war. Tom said he was too tense and too rusty to start law practice. He enrolled in a law refresher course to give him time to settle down to the mundane affairs of civilian life. Tom later became a U.S. attorney and, later still, chief counsel for the N&W Railway at its Roanoke headquarters.

I was sitting with Tom one day at a back table in the large cafeteria on the university "corner." In the front door walked two attractive young ladies. Both were wearing very becoming sweaters. The girls paused momentarily. They cast toothy smiles out over the mostly-male assembly. They then took their place in the food line. I found one of these young ladies particularly

Katherine, as she appeared at my first sight. I became domesticated in short order.

attractive. Her smile was not lost on me. I turned to Tom, who was was well informed on such matters, and asked him if he knew the girl. He told me her name was Katherine Little.

Not long after my first sighting of Katherine, I was on a city bus coming back to the university from downtown. I was seated near the front and noticed Katherine seated toward the rear. When the bus stopped at the university, I got out and waited for her at the curb. When she alighted, I confronted her with the highly original, "Haven't I seen you some place before?" Her reply was an abrupt, "NO!" Undaunted, I asked to walk with her up the sidewalk a ways. During that brief encounter I wangled a date to meet her at the University Commons in the evening.

At the Commons that evening she beat me at ping-pong. Afterwards, I walked her down the long stretch of Rugby Road, to her boardinghouse. She boarded at the home of the Director of Athletics, Tom Carruthers. By coincidence, before the war, I had roomed for a year in the home of Tom Carruthers' father, the Bursar, at 24 East Range on the university grounds. In those days after the war this was enough of an introduction.

Katherine Grizzard Little was from Emporia, Virginia, in the heart of the Peanut and Cotton Belt. She was enrolled at the university in a graduate course in English Literature. She had graduated, at the close of the war, from Randolph-Macon Women's College at Lynchburg, Virginia. Her major there had been philosophy. We found we had each been raised in the Methodist Church.*

Katherine's father, R.W. (Robert William) Little, originally from North Carolina, was a very successful self-made man. He had gained independence and business knowledge as a soldier in World War I. Through hard work and a keen business sense, he had built a thriving business. His Interstate Veneer factory in Emporia manufactured veneer and plywood for packaging. The factory gave employment to many sons of former slaves of the old plantations of the area.

Katherine had grown up taking regular trips with her family to New York, to shop and see plays on the stage. Her father's

*At one time, the Methodists had five schools in Virginia. There was the college for men at Ashland, the women's college at Lynchburg, a boy's high school at Front Royal and another at Bedford, plus a girl's school at Danville (later called Stratford College) and another girl's college at Blackstone, which now serves as a Methodist Conference Center.

Katherine in bridal attire.

business acumen had kept her family comfortable and secure while others were wiped out by the Depression. On her mother's side, whose maiden name was Mary Virginia Grizzard, she was descended from a long line of educated, cultured and accomplished people of Eastern Virginia.

Kind fate brought us together. We set our wedding day for June 6, 1946. We were married at the Methodist Church in Emporia. The reception was held under a large tent surrounded by the spacious lawn and formal gardens of her parent's home. We drove off in an old Packard convertible loaned to us by my father for the occasion.

Our week-long honeymoon was spent by the crystal clear

Cowpasture River, in Bath County, Virginia, in a log cabin retreat owned jointly by Colonel Dillard, Dean Ribble and others. The cabin was located about a mile away from a country store called Deerfield Post Office. For the whole week, we saw no one. Our only companion was an old hound dog we named "Soup," who took care of our dining table scraps. I did all of the cooking and all of the cooking was fried. As soon as we got back home, I came down with the "strep throat." Katherine became my nurse. She also decided she would learn how to cook. She has since become the best cook in the county. She produces cuisine of a high order, all accomplished following the recipes in her varied collection of cookbooks.

After our honeymoon, I moved out of my bachelor's room on the West Lawn. Together, Katherine and I moved into a large downstairs room at Tom Carruther's spacious home on Rugby Road. We lived there until I finished my year's graduate course. In the early fall of 1946 I left for Germany. Katherine went with me as far as New York. In December she joined me in Germany.

Conquerors as Civil Servants

Upon Colonel Dillard's recommendation, I was accepted to serve in the office of General Charles Dailey. He was Chief of Staff for General Lucius Clay, the Military Governor and head of the Office of Military Government for Germany (OMGUS). The office occupied buildings which had formerly been the Luftwaffe's headquarters under the infamous Herman Goering. This was in the Dahlemdorf suburb of the American sector of occupied Berlin.

Our first child was born May 13, 1947, in what had been the Nazi SS (Storm Trooper) headquarters building and barracks. It had been converted into a U.S. military hospital. We named our son, David Hartley, after my father and his mother's father. My father wrote us a long letter about two ancient possible ancestors from Bradford, in Yorkshire, England, named David Hartley. One had been a noted philosopher of his day, one had signed the Treaty of Paris, ending the Revolutionary War, and both had been members of parliament. Therefore, we had picked a winning name.

We lived on Gary Strasse in Dahlem. I could walk to work. This was the heart of the American sector. We had a first rate officers' club, located in the famous old Kaiser Wilhelm Institute. It was here that German scientists invented the U2 missiles which bombed London. Here they had also worked on an atomic bomb, before we beat them to the punch. Our Dahlem neighborhood was filled with the splendid homes of the former German high command and scientists. Now they were all occupied by Americans.

I was one of five Assistant Staff Secretaries serving under Chief Staff Secretary Colonel Charles Hastie, who was under Secretary General, Colonel William Whipple, who was under Brigadier General, Chief of Staff, Charles Dailey, who was Administrative Chief of Staff for Military Governor. General Clay, the son of a Senator from Georgia, was administering the U.S. occupation of Germany just as General Douglas MacArthur was administering our occupation of Japan.

My job, within this system, was to serve as a clearing-house for military government legislation coming up from the American zone of occupation. This included the states of Bavaria, Wuertenberg-Baden and Hesse and the American Sector of Berlin. I was assigned to review legislation prepared by the large Civil Affairs Division. This division was headed first by Ambassador Murphy and then during my time by Dr. Edward Litchfield. Litchfield was later, before his death in an airplane crash, president of the University of Pittsburgh.

After review, the legislation was forwarded to General Clay for approval and enactment into military government law. In matters pertaining to the Civil Affairs Division, all proposed legislation crossed my desk. This was true whether it was coming to or going from General Clay.

All proposals were detailed written studies. If such proposals were not "complete," with all angles covered and answered, I bounced the study back to the division for more complete research. When the proposal originated from General Clay himself, it also passed over my desk to the division and into the field for implementation.

On most Saturday mornings, General Clay held a staff conference. The large central conference room was on the top floor of our headquarters. The building had wings extending from both sides, forming a quadrangle of stone buildings. The conference tables were also arranged in a quadrangle. All the participants, mainly department heads, sat facing each other. General

Clay sat at the center of the head table near the entrance door. Each department head, in turn, briefed, and was briefed by General Clay personally. The general had a most amazing "handle" on the whole range of military government from his Berlin central headquarters.

Our role as military governors was to work ourselves out of a job by gradually turning the government back to the Germans. It was practically impossible for the Germans to understand our principle of civil service. Our Biblical concept of gaining your life as a servant to mankind was obliterated by German militarism. Their system was purely one of rank, lording it over anyone junior to them. Some degree of accommodation was obtained in getting better educated and qualified types to assume the posts in the new "democratic" government of Germany.

The British, French and Russians each occupied separate sectors of the city. These countries had all been devastated by the war. Their occupation forces were forced to live off the land to a great extent. Meanwhile, the commissaries and PXs of the Americans were full of all manner of fresh food and creature comforts. Refrigerated ships and airplanes plied the ocean and airways to bring us this bounty.

Our best friends in Berlin were Jim Raleigh and his wife, from Providence, Rhode Island. He was an assistant staff secretary assigned to the financial division of Military Government. Jim had met his wife in England. She had been a Red Cross worker there when London was under bombing seige during the war. Her nickname was "Buttercup." She and Katherine became best of friends. My fellow staffers invented an equally compatible name for Katherine, "Twinkle-Toes." Together they happily ran around, over the city of Berlin, enjoying the occupation very much. "Buttercup" was a veteran. As they were tooting around Berlin, "Buttercup's" chief admonition to Katherine was, "Stay loose and don't panic."

The Raleighs and Sanders took our holidays together. As a member of the central staff of military government, Jim made all the arrangements. As a result, we went first-class all over Europe. Jim arranged a trip to Copenhagen. There each of us purchased a new Chevrolet car, fresh off the assembly line. Production of new cars had only just resumed, having been halted during the war. We drove the cars back to Berlin. Over the next several months we drove them all over the Alps and around most of Europe. When we departed for home after a year and a half, I sold my car for $2,500, having bought it in Copenhagen for $1,800.

It was a choice thing for the Germans to work for the Americans – plenty of "chockalada and cigaretten" and everything else. A former Whermacht Sergeant, Arthur Stuckart, tall and straight and militarily proficient, attached himself to our home, and to the Raleighs. He was slightly crippled, having made his way back to Berlin from Stalingrad on foot, staying in Russian homes along the way. Arthur regularly served as guide for our wives. Katherine and Buttercup shocked all the German women, as well as the British, French and Russian women, with their agility in going about the city by U-Bahn (Underground Railway) and all other forms of transportation. Arthur and his wife, Hilda, had two children, Wolfgang and Hildegarde.

Our housekeeper, Louisa, spoke several languages. She had worked as a secretary in high offices of German government during the war. She had worked in the very building we now occupied as headquarters. Louisa was a great companion to Katherine.

Louisa's husband had been a petty functionary in the business of following the Nazi troops on the eastern Russian advance. His job was requisitioning food and supplies for the German army from the countryside, through which they were advancing. He was managing the matter of living off the land being invaded. After the war, he was laying low in Berlin. Russian secret agents tracked him down and took him off to Russian imprisonment. His arrest occurred while we were in Germany, and he was out of touch with Louisa. His whereabouts were unknown until a number of years later, when we heard he had returned.

On weekends, Louisa sent her own housekeeper, Frau Krug, to substitute for her at our home, while she went to her own apartment in the central city. On one occasion, Frau Krug was arrested by a German policeman for using Louisa's official permit to ride the American bus. I was called on the telephone by the German police headquarters and the matter was easily dismissed when I explained my position in the chief of staff office. Frau Krug, however, was terrified by the affair. She, indeed, felt herself a member of the servile servant class.

Frau Krug became very attached and loyal to us. When we

left, she cried and had a hard time giving up her fond relationship with our baby boy, David. David always had, and to this date, has an ear for music, after being put to sleep in his German crib by a wonderful German music box at his crib side.

A highlight of our German experience was our membership in the American Church of Berlin whose church edifice, located in the center of the city, had been bombed out. We met in a shared German church opposite the Uncle Tom's U-Bahn Station (Lichtenfeld), which was the next station out from Dahlem, toward the Grunewald Forest of Hansel and Gretel fairy tale fame. The American Church was interdenominational and our preacher was Dr. Arthur Siebens.

Dr. Siebens was a Presbyterian. Before coming to Germany, he had headed up a special commission that had broken up a ring of political corruption in a large city in Ohio. He had helped obtain indictments and convictions of the corrupt forces which had bribed to control both political parties. The prosecution resulted in the imprisonment of some very powerful people. After that, Ohio was not considered a safe place for him. So, this large and impressive former football hero took on the job of reviving the bombed-out American church in Berlin. There he baptized our child, David.

I was on his church board, along with such men as my good friend, Ben Habberton, lawyer from Texas, political affairs section of the Civil Affairs Division; Ambassador William Heath, and others.

We were able to obtain some aid for the American church through our several U.S. senators and congressmen. One was Congressman Judd of Minnesota, who had a strong church and foreign missions background. Another was my senator, Harley Kilgore. Senator Kilgore had, in his private office in the U.S. capitol, about the largest brass spittoon that I have ever beheld. He punctuated our visit there by frequently spitting into the thing.

There were a great many talented Americans living in Germany during the occupation period. Many would go on to make a name for themselves later. We had a wonderful circle of friends and did considerable socializing.

One evening we had fellow Staff Secretary, Ted Boydton over to dinner. After the meal, Katherine served cherry pie for dessert. Not yet the accomplished cook she is today, she had failed to remove the pits from the cherries. As he discovered the first pit, Ted's diplomatic inquiry was, "Is this olive pie?"

One of my closest friends in the staff center was Dr. Harry Franklin. He was a special advisor to the military governor. Dr. Franklin was a veritable walking encyclopedia of German history. After we returned home, he and his wife visited us and he spoke at our local Rotary Club luncheon.

Some of our friends, like us, had children born abroad, or had been born abroad to American parents, working in the foreign service. Under the U.S. Constitution, only native born citizens are qualified to become president of the United States. These friends, and our son David, were excluded by this provision. I later wrote my U.S. Senator, Chapman Revercomb, to initiate a change in this aspect of the Constitution. He did not choose to tackle the job. I feel that some day this must be done. We live in an intimate community of nations in a smaller world.

Katherine received good attention from the American, British, French and Germans in our mixing and mingling and going to the opera and other events in all sectors of Berlin. The Russians lived in their own, separate dull world apart. The only contribution they would offer in the constant quadripartite meetings was a blunt, "Nyet."

Katherine's good looks and her good, American-style attire set her apart. A certain German artist wanted to paint her. I consented to his many visits to our home, while Katherine "sat" for his art work. The end result was a large (about two and one half by three feet) oil on canvas, with a gold frame. The likeness was good, but he put her in a costume that looked like Italian Renaissance.

I don't remember what I paid the artist, but it was probably in cigarettes, which was the real currency of the day in Berlin anyway. We didn't smoke, so our cigarette allotment was ready money for such native art work, as well as some wonderful German china, acquired from time to time.

We decided we didn't like the oil painting and gave it to our housekeeper, Louisa. Years later, at home in West Virginia, we decided we would like to have the painting, especially since our parents were anxious to see it. We wrote to Louisa and asked to buy it, but she wouldn't part company with it for love nor money. So, the painting is somewhere in Berlin, we know not where, maybe in some fine home posing as an ancient Italian painting of priceless value.

The role played by the United States in World War II and its aftermath has to be the greatest, and noblest accomplishment in all world history. We had desperately fought two wars, at the same time, on opposite sides of the world. Then, in victory, we occupied and rehabilitated each of our defeated enemies. General Clay and General MacArthur, each accomplished their missions with great efficiency, effectiveness and compassion. America, thereby, helped set the stage for a promising new world order. I was proud to have a small hand in this historic accomplishment.

My military government staff experience has helped me in all of my law practice and office management. The post-war government of the United States has profited greatly by the experience of administering these two occupations. They served as prototypes for our own bureaucracy. War has many useful by-products for the betterment of mankind.

The dismantling of the Soviet Union and the Communist world, is a direct result of our positive, rehabilitative style of military occupation. Especially when compared with the purely negative occupation policies pursued by the Soviet Union.

My involvement in post-war rehabilitation gave me hope for a better world and a more unified world, as foretold by the poet Alfred Lord Tennyson in 1842 in his poem *Locksley Hall:*

For I dipt into the future, far as human eye could see,
Saw the Vision of the world, and all the wonder that would be;
Saw the heavens fill with commerce, argosies of magic sails,
Pilots of the purple twilight, dropping down with costly bales;
Heard the heavens fill with shouting, and there rain'd a ghastly
dew
From the nations' airy navies grappling in the central blue;
Far along the world-wide whisper of the south-wind rushing
warm,
With the standards of the peoples plunging thro'the thunderstorm;
Till the war-drum throbb'd no longer, and the battle-flags were
furl'd
In the Parliament of man, the Federation of the world.
There the common sense of most shall hold a fretful realm in
awe,
And the kindly earth shall slumber, lapt in universal law.

COURTHOUSES AND CAUSES IN SOUTHERN WEST VIRGINIA

The Practice and Other Skirmishes

My war experiences, education, and work with the military government all led me to focus on a career in government service, with my job in Germany a prelude. I was offered a State Department position in the section of Wildlife and Fisheries, writing treaties to regulate international uses of the Atlantic. My civil service rating was to be a P-11. This would open advancement into top level State Department posts on the world scene.

However, my father was writing letters to me which were becoming increasingly poignant, wanting to see his grandson. My parents had lost their most gifted and most promising daughter, Sarah, a few years before the war. They had put me through college and law school under great financial strain following the Great Depression and had endured the years of war's uncertainty and, now, I could read great nostalgia in my father's letters, sent to me in Germany. My parents wanted to see their first grandson, David Hartley.

We cut short our government service and returned to West Virginia realizing my father needed me in his practice. We went back to Princeton and to my father's law practice.

Upon our return we took up residence with my parents until I could get established. They were living in the very imposing, white columned home we called "The Big House." It had been built by Lowry G. Bowling who had been the clerk of the county court just about forever. The house, which sat on three acres, was now owned by Dr. I.T. Peters. The same Dr. Peters who had earlier rented the Blake house to my parents after Daddy's bankruptcy. Our second child Mary Hylton Sanders was born, October 3, 1949, while we lived in this house.

Home in the Allegheny mountains of southern West Virginia, I studied to take the West Virginia Bar, having passed the Virginia Bar six years earlier but failing to be introduced to the Virginia Supreme Court in the haste to get into the war. Thus, reciprocity (five years) had not even started to run to qualify me to practice in West Virginia.

It was good, nevertheless, to study the West Virginia Code of Laws and case decisions to get me launched as a West Virginia lawyer. I passed the "substantive" half of the bar exam and failed the "procedural" half the first go'round and had to pass the "procedural" exam at a second session six months later.

I also used the time upon my return to Princeton to write and prepare my thesis on military government, to satisfy Colonel Dillard and my degree requirements. I submitted the manuscript, which had been typed by my father's secretary. Based upon my year of study, my year abroad in the military government and my thesis, I was awarded a degree.

I was the first person ever to earn a Masters Degree in International Law from the University of Virginia. Graduation was held in June 1948 at Charlottesville. Not knowing where else to place me, I marched first in the cap and gown procession, right after all the faculty, ahead of all the other degree recipients of all departments. I proudly marched through the heart of Mr. Jefferson's planned university. Starting at the Rotunda, the procession marched down the length of the central lawn to the convocation at Cabell Hall.

I recently received the 1995 Directory of the University of Virginia Law School Association. It listed over four hundred women and men from throughout the world who have earned their Master of Law degrees in International Law at Charlottesville. The Association has sponsored reunions of the graduates in Oxford, Bruges, Charlottesville, Vienna and, in June 1995, in Athens, Greece. The International Law Degree program had its humble origin with my application on return from the Pacific Theater of War, 1945-1946.

And, so, with my Masters Degree and West Virginia law license in hand, I launched upon the country practice of law, with my father. I was his first and only partner. It was as if he had kept the position open for me all of his life. We were 50/50, as Sanders & Sanders. Our office was in front on the third (top) floor of the Princeton Bank & Trust building across Main Street from the courthouse.

Katherine's father came to visit us in Princeton. He had purchased homes for his two other children. He offered to buy us a stately house on Walker Street. It had been built by lawyer Albert W. Reynolds, first general counsel for the Norfolk & Western Railway. Katherine, who was very pregnant at the time, felt the house wasn't exactly to her liking. So, in spite of the fact that Mr. Little had his checkbook out and was ready to pay cash for the house, we passed it up. Mr. Little died soon thereafter. A number of years later we would build a new home outside town, using a great portion of Katherine's inheritance.

It soon became apparent that my father was suffering from a brain tumor. I took him to his old university and the Hospital at Charlottesville. Famous brain surgeon Dr. Gayle Crutchfield, allowed me to don a white uniform, skull cap and mask and to remain in the operating room. Only Novocain, a local anesthetic, was used while the doctor suctioned off the *glio blastoma* tumor from the right rear lobe of the brain. I held my father's hand and reassured him during the three-hour procedure.

Dr. Crutchfield told me that he hoped he had gotten it all but, he warned, it was virtually impossible to remove all traces of such a virile cancer of the brain. In fact there were no cases of a complete cure on record. So, in spite of the fact the doctor found my father to have the physical system of a much younger man, a one year survival was the most that could be expected. As it turned out, my father and I would have four more years together.

Just as my parents had to vacate the Blake residence when Dr. Peters decided to sell it, we were forced to move from the"Big House" when Dr. Peters' widow decided to sell. Katherine and I purchased a small new home in town on Henry Street for my parents. We bought ourselves an old two-story brick home on Mahood Avenue, a few blocks northwest of the courthouse. Our third child, Katherine Todd Sanders, was born while we lived here, on May 9, 1952.

As I entered into the practice of law in the hills of southern West Virginia, I got my bearings from my father. My basic law school training was now years in the past, a war away. My father was able to give me good grounding and insightful instructions into the fundamentals of law practice and client relationship.

In the first years I would sit at counsel table with my father in his trials. His forty-five years of practice and his integrity had created a great good name and a large number of faithful clients.

The front windows of our three-room, third-floor office had, blazoned in gold bordered silver letters, first *"Hartley Sanders"* and then after my arrival, *"Sanders and Sanders, Attorneys."* Below the windows of our office the trolley line from the Virginian Railway station a mile away on Mercer Street met the trolley lines to Bluefield and the larger Norfolk and Western Station.

My personal office was small, with windows on an alley and three doors; one to the hall, one to the reception room and one to my father's office in front overlooking the trolleys and courthouse. My room was also the library. These three rooms had constituted my father's office since his arrival in town in 1907. I soon revised the filing system and my father joked that his old system was like a barrel where he could reach down into the barrel and always find what he wanted. Now, he complained, the system was a maze.

After three years my father required a second brain operation, this time under general anesthesia. He returned to the practice for a year afterwards. He still walked one mile to work, one mile back at lunch, one mile home at evening, – four miles a day, until the last week of his life when he stayed at home. Even then, he dressed and shaved every day and sat in his rocking chair at his front window consulting my inherited gold vest pocket watch, waiting for my arrival and for me to summarize the day at the office. And, as always, he wore a coat and tie every day.

In the evening of his last day, he went to his room and fell into a coma. He was transported to the hosptial, where he died that night. I kissed him goodnight as he left his rocking chair and went to his bed that last night of his life. The year was 1952.

My parents had sent me to my father's schools and had suffered through the lean years of the depression and the war – my duty was clear – I should continue his practice. My personal ambition for a larger future in the international community was abandoned. Most of my contemporaries had moved away to larger opportunities in larger communities. I resigned myself to making the most of my country practice. Ever since, I have studied the countryside, the history and the families as the basis of my practice, building on the base provided by my father's practice and reputation.

Thus, I inherited my father's practice.

The fact that I had matured as a marine line officer in the Pacific War, and as a staff officer in the U.S. Military Government in Germany, gave me certain confidence and a certain appeal to a country clientele back home. My father's example and advice gave me assurance and direction in the courtroom and in law office management and in right relationship with country clients.

When Hartley went bankrupt in the great depression he bankrupted a large debt at the Athens Bank. Afterwards he re-assumed that debt and was paying it off by sharing one half of his fees each time he searched titles and prepared the papers for the bank's loans. After my father's death I continued to pay off his debt for twelve years. Upon completion, I told the bank I wanted to surrender such representation in favor of more time in court for trials instead of searching the land records. I received a nice letter of appreciation from Bank President Fred Cooper.

After my father's death I acquired the adjoining front office where the Bluefield newspaperman "Skeeter" Anderson had sat for years with his Remington typewriter, very much in touch with this center of activity at the courthouse – town bank and trolley terminals. Most of his news was garnered at the courthouse clerks office and the courtrooms where publicly attended trials were conducted. Two justices of the peace offices and miniature courtrooms for small trials also were located in the courthouse square array of buildings. Another justice of the peace held sway in Bluefield.

I knocked a door through to the new room and started the long process of hiring law associates to carry the growing client load. I started off with Johnny Dean, my old First Sergeant of Marines, who left shortly before my father's death. He had married his navy nurse after he lost an eye at the battle of Okinawha. They went back to California.

A few years after my father's death I acquired the remaining two offices of the front of the third floor. I got the front corner rooms of Mr. W.H. Dangerfield, business lawyer and president of the downtown Commercial Bank, when he died. With this seven-room suite, I began hiring or associating new lawyers, attempting to build a firm. I first associated Ben White as *"Sanders & White."*

I had recently acquired the business of defending automobile insuance and quickly became a very busy lawyer, thanks to John R. Pendleton.

John R. Pendleton was attorney for the railroad and represented State Farm Insurance. Our two families were friends. His older brother, Ben Pendleton, was the partner of James W. Hale, a landmark law firm, as *"Hale and Pendleton."* Their fa-

133

ther, David Pendleton, came to the area from Falls Church in Fairfax County and served as "Latin teacher" to the early county lawyers and leaders.

John R. Pendleton had the two corner rooms on the second floor over the bank by the clock. He was the only lawyer in the county seat who had the Federal Reporters (Federal Court decisions). I spent time in his office consulting the federal case precedents. Before John R. Pendleton's death he had recommended me to the State Farm Insurance Company. After his death they gave me their business.

When I was young at the bar half the people didn't carry auto insurance. Juries would always concern themselves with whether the defendant was insured, even though under the case law the fact was not disclosed. It was reversible error for either counsel to divulge the presence or absence of insurance in a case. The juries, nevertheless, spent much of their time trying to decide whether there was insurance involved. I am sure I won some cases because the jury figured my client was not insured; sure that an insurance company would not hire such a young lawyer to represent them. Juries didn't want a fellow citizen to have to pay a verdict out of his own pocket or take the shirt off his back.

Secretaries

Through the years, I had seen that changing secretaries was a major event in my father's solo practice. A secretary would leave after having been well trained by my father. This was for various reasons; moving away, a government job, better pay, and often without much notice. He would then be confronted with finding a substitute in a hurry, or training a new secretary from scratch.

My father had a practice of interviewing a new secretary by asking whether she had studied Latin, which would indicate she knew something about words. He trained some of his best secretaries right out of high school. Many of his longest term secretaries came from the outlying countryside. Some came from homes that did not practice speaking the King's English. Some from homes that didn't speak anything resembling the English language. The spoken word at home was vastly different from the written word in a law office. Many of our best secretaries were "bilingualists", using different "languages" at home and

134

the office.

Through the years I learned to hire girls from the country-side and small schools, rather than girls from the larger schools, towns or cities who thought too highly of themselves. Invariably, the girls from modest backgrounds were better satisfied, more loyal and longer lasting, even if they reverted to their home-spun version of the language when they went home.

My father's secretary, at the time I joined him, had been trained from scratch and had advanced fast. She had great native intelligence. She had been alert enough to get her parents a nice home at an estate auction sale. She ended up marrying a college engineering graduate and moved with him to South Carolina where he had gotten a good job. She raised a family there, entered into church and civic life and became a leading citizen of the place. Still, her basic language remained West Virginia Mountainese.

One of my father's best secretaries was "Miss" Ruth Cook. He had hired her at age sixteen and trained her. "Miss" Ruth's training and ability set her above the rest and gave her independence in her profession. She graduated to court reporting and to the best paying jobs in the area. She became a living legend in the secretarial and court reporting community.

When my father died, she was winding down her long legal career. Without being asked, she came to our home and took charge of funeral arrangements. Promptly after the funeral, she volunteered her legal secretarial services to me. For quite a few years, she became my chief secretary. I could give Miss Ruth a day's work in five minutes of instruction at the start of the day, leaving me free to go to court and prepare my cases. She helped train younger secretaries.

I soon started hiring more than one secretary and always had backup secretaries in training so I wouldn't experience the secretarial ordeals that my father experienced. I thought it better to hire several, train several and keep the best. The secretaries began training the secretaries.

Some of the best secretaries had intimate relationships with their lawyer bosses. Everyone in town knew. Those lawyers didn't experience the agony that my father did. My father said that these secretaries had become permanent fixtures, because they had been attached to their desks (but he didn't put it quite that way.) My mother certainly would never have tolerated such an arrangement. Modern-day laws make such relationships archaic and actionable.

In the summer of 1996, as my son David and I were driving through the Wyoming County coalfields, taking photographs for this book, he recalled driving with me in the early days of my practice. I then defended State Farm in their automobile liability cases in my home county of Mercer as well as Wyoming, Logan, McDowell and other southern counties. Those were the days – the 1950s and 1960s. Thirteen years of defending State Farm cases in the coalfields. I wore out several cars winding around the two-lane mountain roads of southern West Virginia.

He remembered going with me as I sought out witnesses at their homes. How I would write out their "statement of facts" in my handwriting on yellow legal pads. How I would then read it back to them and each of us sign and date every page. I would put this in my briefcase, thank them and be on my way.

This was prior to the procedural changes called the pretrial discovery process by which you pin-down the evidence by depostions of the parties and the witnesses. I did my own first-hand discovery in the field. It was with this firsthand knowledge of the scene and the witnesses that I tried my cases. In fact this personal investigation made the cases come alive for me and provided motivation.

In the early years I had many, many partners and associates, most for a short time. I could teach them all I knew in two years. After two years most of them would leave, feeling they knew enough to start their own practices. Later, when southern West Virginia acquired Interstate highways, bypasses, shopping malls and modern hospitals, my law associates became more interested in taking-up permanent residence, as opposed to just acquiring experience and moving on.

With the liberal trend towards more insurance coverage and higher verdicts I reassessed my position. In my years as a defense lawyer I had worked harder, prepared better and tried more cases than the lawyers I was coming up against. By switching to the plaintiff's side I could use this same hard work to make a better life for myself and my family. Instead of billing an insurance company by the hour, I would represent clients for a percentage fee, contingent upon any recovery I could win for them. This act of sharing in the fate and outcome of a case made a client's cause an even more urgent and personal matter.

My Father's Partner

One of the first cases I assisted my father with, in our five years together, was a claim by William Frederick Carr. A native of the New River area of Mercer County, Carr had one of the best backwoodsmen accents I ever heard. He had taken care of an old man named Clemons, who lived alone way back in the country. The man's children had declined to take care of him in his old age and he had no one else. Carr moved in and took care of this invalid in his prolonged last illness, under the promise by the old man to compensate him. There were crudely written promises by the old man. We brought a claim for reasonable services against the estate, which consisted mainly of the old man's home and small acreage.

One of our main witnesses, to prove the extent and nature of services rendered, was a young man who loafed about the place and who was known to be a frequent user of alcohol and a carouser. His name was Bill Ingram. He was about my age and without any plans or direction for his life. Bill was one of fourteen children of the Dewey Ingram family.

We were sure that opposing counsel was going to try to discredit this witness as a roustabout and an alcoholic. Therefore, we briefed the witness and advised him to tell the whole truth about his habits because that was not the real issue in the case. On direct examination he gave very effective testimony in favor of our claim. On cross examination, opposing counsel asked Bill if he was rather fond of alcoholic beverages. Bill unhesitatingly and freely confessed that he never refused a drink and drank about everything he could get his hands on. This confession was good for his soul and it proved his truthfulness as to the nature of the nursing/housekeeping services rendered by our client. We won the case accordingly.

Fred Carr, and Bill Ingram and his father, in fact the whole Ingram family, became my staunch clients. Bill took a new lease on life and quit his drinking. He later went away to a northern city and held down a good long-term job.

That particular corner of the county has sent me many good cases since that time, including several from the Ingram family, fourteen children strong. Mrs. Ingram, a member of the old Melvin family, was a very good-looking woman. Dewey kept her at home in a perpetual state of pregnancy. One of her pretty daughters married a state trooper. It seemed the family became a closer and happier family after Bill mended his ways. Recently, in one of the latest such cases from this same place, we represented a young widow suing over the death of her husband. He had been a heavy equipment operator. He had worked in a quarry loading limestone into the trucks. The trucks then took the stone to a grinding mill which reduced it to gravel.

The quarry's floor contained numerous dynamite charges which had been placed but had failed to discharge. The company knew this, yet they proceeded with quarry operations despite the obvious danger. One day unexpectedly, one of these hidden charges went off. A high cliff overhanging the quarry floor was jarred loose, sending huge boulders on the floor below. One struck the large shovel being operated by our client's young husband. He was killed instantly.

We recovered a large sum of money, over and above the workers' compensation benefits, because we were able to prove the wilful, wanton, deliberate and gross negligence of the quarry owner. Early goodwill in this particular community brought many such cases to my office door.

FIRST YEARS
AT THE BAR
OF JUSTICE

Criminal Law and the Defense

After the death of my father in 1952, I took on a number of colorful murder cases and other criminal matters. These trials made much better news headlines than civil damage lawsuits. Thus they built a young lawyer's public reputation and ability to attract clients. I assisted the prosecution in five of the nine or so murder trials in which I was involved. In these cases I had been hired by the deceased's family to obtain justice. This role is termed a "special prosecutor." The regular-elected prosecutor was, more often than not, very happy to have such assistance and, generally, let the special prosecutor carry the load. This practice has died out with the large staff of lawyers the prosecutors now have.

Rape Case

I defended several rape cases. One of the most interesting was for a fellow named John Johnson, who lived in a McComas coal camp at the head of Red Dog Hollow. He was charged with raping his nearest neighbor's wife. John had a wife and nine kids of his own. He was sure that he had a good alibi and could prove that he could not possibly have been in his neighbor's home at the time of the alleged rape, which was very early in the morning, when the mine shift was changing.

He could not raise bond. Therefore, he remained incarcerated and I had to interview him in the jail conference room as I prepared his case. I could detect that he was not being truthful with me with his story about the alibi but I could not break him down.

I contacted the young camp doctor, Leith-Hartman, who had a fine reputation among the miners for using his Jeep, and sometime his horse, to make house calls at some of their remote homes. I brought this young doctor into the jail conference room with me and told John that I did not think he was telling me the truth. The doctor felt as I did and told my client that if he was not telling his lawyer the truth, he was digging his own grave. John confessed that he had been telling a story.

This necessitated an interesting shift in trial strategy.

By this time the prosecution had rested its case and we were already putting on our case. Up until then we had been proceeding on John's theory of alibi in the trial. This was based on a time element which seemed to make it impossible that he could have taken the time to rape his neighbor's wife on the way to work that morning. We proved from his wife the time he left his home. We had shown that he clocked in at the lamp house, about a mile down the hollow, and commenced to work.

The prosecution, and the jury, felt we were attempting to establish such an alibi until the last day of the trial. Then, to the great surprise of the opposition, we decided to put John on the stand and go for the truth of the matter.

The fact was, John had intercourse with this woman that morning, and this was nothing new. Their relationship had a long history. They had established prearranged signals. When her husband departed down the hollow to go to work, she would turn on her porch light as a signal to John. He would then go to the rear of her house and come in through the bedroom window. Thus, they would proceed with their pleasure before he went down the hollow and started to work. All of this came out as John testified assuredly about these matters.

I arranged for his wife to sit stoically in the courtroom on the front row and listen to this story. It took considerable woodshedding, persuasion and reassurance to convince her to sit in silence through that testimony. Some of their numerous and well-behaved children also appeared in the courtroom. The "victim," the prosecution's main witness, along with her father who had urged her on throughout the trial, seemed to slink in their seats. The tide turned rapidly in our favor.

John came out on solid ground. In victory he was a hero. He was even accepted so by his wife. They continued living happily together along with their house full of children.

Murder in the Family

A good client is a lawyer's best asset. Such a client was Richard Carrington. He was a very bright young black man, with a wife and two children. His old widowed mother came to see me from nearby Tazewell County, Virginia. She had mortgaged her home to employ me, with a cash fee, to represent her son.

Richard had killed his mother-in-law's boyfriend. The mother-in-law and her boyfriend had a habit of coming to

Richard's apartment in Bluefield when he and his wife were away to a movie or such. They would have a party while Richard and his wife were out. They would clean out the icebox and would drink "white lightning." White lightning was a liquid produced by burning certain "canned heat" substances. It made a pretty rank concoction which, although it was very dangerous to drink, produced a very quick high.

We were able to prove these actions of the mother-in-law and the deceased. We proved that Richard had come home to the apartment with his wife, only to find that this couple had once again depleted his family's groceries. Then he finally flew off the handle and drew a pocket knife. After he and his mother-in-law's boyfriend had engaged in a strong argument, he stabbed the man one time in the heart and killed him. It was a plain case of good riddance of a bum usurper of Richard's larder.

Richard made a fine witness. He took the stand after considerable review or "woodshedding." He was to tell the whole truth and nothing but the truth. He pulled out his neatly laundered white handkerchief and cried very beautifully during the trial. He made a most effective witness. He was a high caliber performer and reminds me of the actor Eddie Murphy, who makes all kinds of money in Hollywood these days. The jury acquitted him in short order. After their verdict was announced he promptly went down the row of jurors, shook hands with each one and thanked them personally.

We developed quite a rapport during the trial. For several years later, no matter where he was, Richard would call me on the telephone long distance. In one call he told me he attained the rank of colonel. He called to report other successes. He kept in touch with me because we had become such good friends and allies during his trial. The calls were often at holiday time and were generally in the evenings. The circumstances suggested that he might have been socializing a little bit and might have wanted to impress his friends.

That's the way it goes in the plaintiff's practice. You get very close to your clients as a country trial lawyer.

A lawyer has in his charge the social identity of the client. Whereas doctors treat the physical and preachers address the spiritual, it's a person's social identity that is really at stake in the arena of a trial at law. This is the client's most priceless possession, often more important than life itself. Without a social identity, we are nothing. This is the basis of all of our striving – steal my money, you steal trash; steal my reputation and you are on serious ground. This is all the more the case for the true mountaineer who has little else to lose but his reputation.

Murder of Husband

Another interesting criminal case contributed to my early reputation as a lawyer. This was my defense of a very attractive young female. She was a light-skinned black woman and had formerly been one of "the girls" in the famous "Cinder Bottom" area of Keystone. Keystone was in the coal county of McDowell. In the heyday of coal mining in that county "Cinder Bottom" was infamous for wide open prostitution and gambling.

Alice employed me to defend her upon the charge of killing her husband, Jay.

I had known Jay and his family very well when growing up in our town. Alice had retired from the notorious cinder bottom prostitution trade and had married my old friend. Alice and Jay lived on "colored hill" in Princeton. He and Alice were pillars of the church. Jay had children by an ex-wife named Mildred, who lived in town. Mildred was also a strong church member.

Jay had the duty of providing for his ex-wife and their children. Jay's family were premier hog raisers in the town from my earliest days. Jay supplemented his railroad income by continuing his hog farming. He often shared hams with his ex-wife. He would visit her and take one half of the ham and take the other half back home. Alice took exception to this practice. She also felt, with some justification it appears, that he was tarrying too long with these ham deliveries.

Alice confronted Jay about this one day on High Street at the edge of the black community. They got into a heated argument over the matter. Alice brought a pocket knife from her purse and stabbed Jay one time in the heart and killed him. Apparently, she threw the knife over in the bushes on the side of the road. The prosecutor was not a Matlock or a Perry Mason and did not find the knife. (This was before metal detectors.) He could not produce the death weapon at the trial. Not having a weapon is always hurtful to the prosecution's case.

During the trial, Alice made a very excellent witness. She

expressed great grief over the loss of her fine husband, who was well known and respected by everybody in the community. Woodshedding and rehearsal of her testimony was not neglected by me. I was able to find out the whole truth of her defense and was able to put it on effectively, with such an appealing witness, that the jury acquitted her and she walked out of the courtroom a free woman.

I heard from her by Christmas cards for many years. She moved away from the community shortly after the trail. She had lost her new found way of life and was the real loser in the matter. Alice was a quality person and very much like another southern West Virginian, Blaze Star, who was the mistress of Governor Earl Long of Louisiana. Like Blaze Star, Alice did not have many opportunities open to her for economic survival equal to her God-given talents of pure good looks and high intelligence. I was most sympathetic in her defense.

Woodshedding

The practice of country plaintiff's law is rewarding and often results in lifetime friendships. And often, one satisfied client tells another of your merit as a lawyer.

All clients and all witnesses need and deserve woodshedding and dress rehearsal. You should undertake that process at the first interview and before they encounter opposition counsel, which means before the discovery process, which is now the name of the game in trial practice these days.

If you fail to know the whole truth, and fail to woodshed your witnesses before the fishing expedition by the opposite side begins, you can lose the war very early in the game. The more educated your client or witness is, the more he may need woodshedding to overcome his own conceit and to give him caution in the strange process of trial.

Expert witnesses need woodshedding as badly as anybody. They are very deprived when they do not get needed rehearsals. As a matter of fact, most expert witnesses, be they medical or scientific or whatever, realize that there are two sides to every case. There are a lot of experts, enough to take opposite views on almost any subject. Your expert needs to fully realize the nature of the contest. He does not want to end up looking bad because it could affect his future credentials to be on the losing side. Therefore, it behooves counsel to spend a lot of time with the expert so that the witness realizes that counsel understands the subject and knows how to do his part in presenting the evidence. This gives the expert enough confidence to stick by his guns and make a strong impression on the jury. One of the main purposes of such "woodshedding" rehearsals is to get your witness prepared for the skillful and cunning onslaught of your worthy adversary.

One of the adversary's favorite tricks is baiting your client or witness on cross-examination by his leading question. The adversary tries to appear to the witness as a nice person and wants the witness to agree with his suggestions. Your client or witness must know in advance that the lawyer for the other side has his bread buttered by them and he should beware of such sweetness and honey by way of cross-examination.

It is as much a dereliction of your duty to fail to lead a witness on cross-examination as it is to lead your own witness on direct examination. In other words, your witness must tell his story without suggestions; whereas, you must cross-examine the adverse witness on the basis of leading questions. This is a hard rule for a young beginning lawyer to understand. However the

Mercer County Courthouse at Princeton.

young lawyer will not have much success until he does understand this rule of examining witnesses.

The trial of a lawsuit is very much like a stage play and the lawyer is the producer and has to put the play on in proper sequence and know his witnesses stories well in advance of the skirmish.

The Several Careers
of Judge Bailey

Judge R.D. Bailey was tall and full bodied, with sparse sandy hair. He was of a kind and even temper. Totally and calmly in control, he was the political boss of Wyoming County. He had first served as county prosecutor for years and had an office in the courthouse. Later, he was elected circuit judge of Wyoming County and moved to another office in the same courthouse. At the conclusion of his career as judge, he managed to keep an office in the courthouse. From that location he practiced law and continued to run the county.

As I remember from my early law days, all the leading old-time lawyers, when visiting another lawyer, would always exchange a few tall tales first. Never in a hurry, they would gradually get around to the purpose of the visit. It would have seemed rude otherwise. A great mutual respect and camaraderie existed among the lawyers.

I had the pleasure of opposing the genial yet formidible ex-judge while I was defending State Farm Insurance in several cases. On a number of occasions I visited his office on the first floor of the courthouse. We would sit and visit a spell before getting to the point of the meeting. In these easy-going conferences we were able to sound out the strength or weaknesses of each other's case. Often we could reach a fair settlement by this method.

On several of my visits with the judge, we were interrupted by phone calls seeking his endorsement for some sort of a job or another. His endorsement was quite apparently a prerequisite for most any job in the county.

One such case involved an automobile collision on Route 10 between Mullens, Ittman and Pineville. The judge's client, the plaintiff, claimed he was the injured passenger in a two-car collision. I represented the insured driver of the other car. The wreck happened on a curve in front of a house belonging to an old couple. The husband was a retired coal miner. They enjoyed their quiet home and nice vegetable garden. The walls of their home were liberally adorned with pictures of Jesus Christ and various prayers and religious quotations.

They had heard the crash in front of their peaceful home and went immediately to the scene. I had heard rumors that they knew Judge Bailey's client had switched his seat at the driver's wheel with his buddy who was the real passenger. The plaintiff had been drinking alcohol and was thus driving under the influence.

It took a lot of exhortation on my part, upon visiting the old folks in their home, that the religion they professed required them to tell the truth and the whole truth. At length, I convinced them of their duty to testify in the pending lawsuit.

I'm sure it was a revelation to the politically active ex-judge when I told him the true state of the facts. The case was disposed of quickly, and very reasonably.

While Judge Bailey was the genial boss of Wyoming County politics, it was the three Christie brothers, lawyers Sidney and Sam, and their younger brother, all major bankers in "wild and wooly" Keystone, who ran McDowell County. It had been this way since the Roosevelt administration.

In another Wyoming County case Judge Bailey represented the injured mother of the secretary of Sam Christie.

My client was Robert Lusk, a teenager from the Wyoming County village of Matheny. Young Lusk's father was a coal miner during the week. On the weekends he was well known as a barber and would cut other miner's hair in his home. He had several children, including another son a year or so younger than my defendant. My client and his younger brother enjoyed helping me investigate the accident.

By the time of trial Robert Lusk was in the U.S. Air Force, stationed in Colorado. I had him flown in the day before the trial to sit at counsel table with me in his neat blue Air Force uniform. He testified that in the accident, which occurred at dusk, he simply did not see the other car approaching. He admitted that he was partially on the wrong side of the road when the collision occurred.

The trial lasted several days due to the extensive evidence

concerning injuries and treatment of the plaintiff. Instead of sitting in the courtroom beside her well-known lawyers, Judge Bailey and Sam Christie, the dignified old lady plaintiff spent much of trial resting comfortably in a back room. Throughout the trial, my young client's barber/miner father and his humble mother sat on the front row. His mother fidgeted and wrung her white handkerchief in a state of subdued anxiety.

The jury rendered its verdict for the plaintiff, but in such a low amount that the plaintiff's attorneys asked for a new trial. A conference was called in the judge's chambers immediately following the jury verdict. Trial Judge Robert Worrell observed that he saw no legal grounds for granting a new trial but, he was going to cancel his policy with State Farm Insurance since the verdict was so low and inadequate.

Both of the Lusk boys went to college and law school and one of them ended up as a claim adjuster for an insurance company.

Wyoming County Courthouse at Pineville.

A Timely Prayer

A short time before I quit working on the defense side, I was employed by State Farm to defend the newlywed son of one of my old high school classmates.

The boy's name was Freddie. He was one of many children who had grown up on the old line farm family. His father, my classmate, had dropped out of high school and worked at the Virginian Railway's Princeton shops. He had raised a large family on his cattle farm in the Green Valley area, between Princeton and Bluefield.

The son, Freddie, was starting out his married life as a barber and his pretty wife was a beautician. The couple had an apartment just off the main highway, along the straight stretch through the community of Green Valley.

Freddie left that apartment late one afternoon to go down the highway to a small store for a loaf of bread, while his bride was making supper. As he reached the mid-point of the straight stretch, he turned left across the road and into the parking lot of the grocery store.

He had checked for oncoming traffic before he turned to go across. Just as he stopped his car in the parking lot, there was a terrible crash. A car had been coming from the opposite direction at a high rate of speed. It had crossed the center line and collided head-on into a car carrying three women that had been following Freddie. This violent collision instantly killed two of the women, who were elderly ladies of a prominent family. The third woman, Miss Mary Brown, was horribly injured and disfigured in the crash and the fire that followed.

Middle-aged Miss Mary worked in a Princeton bank. She was a well-respected old maid. She was also one of the members of the Methodist Sunday School class I was teaching at the time. Her father, who had owned a small dairy farm on the Old Athens Road, north of Princeton, had been a friend of my father.

The families of the deceased sisters had settled their claims with the insurance companies. Miss Mary, who had been a passenger, brought suit for an astronomical sum of money for her terrible injuries. She hired Walter Burton, the "big gun" plaintiff's lawyer of the area. State Farm hired me to defend this case which would come on for trial in circuit court, in my hometown.

Walter Burton and I were frequently adversaries and were

never allies. However, we each had offices on the top floor of the "Law Building," across from the courthouse.

I prepared the defense with much diligence. I spent hours conducting long interviews with my client, Freddie, and his wife. His wife was to testify as a witness at the trial. I worked with them so that they would be well prepared for the assault this "big gun" lawyer would wage against them. Their young reputation in the community, where they had just started out their married life, was literally on the line.

The driver and passengers of the other car were boys from Black Oak Mountain. I knew of their families. I fully investigated the background of these young men and interviewed many of their neighbors. By the time of the trial I had developed all the details of the accident and the events leading up to it.

The young driver was home on leave from the navy. He, his brother and a neighbor had been drinking and carousing around the county all that weekend. They were flying high down the straightway at the time of the collision. The long skid marks left by their car showed their great speed. They had veered into the oncoming lane of traffic just before colliding with the other vehicle.

At trial Freddie tesitifed he had passed off the road and was getting out of his car as the collision occurred. He stated he had seen no approaching traffic, within reasonable proximity, on that heavily-traveled roadway. After the crash, he saw that other vehicles were stopping at the scene and that a crowd was gathering. Freddie was overwhelmed, frightened, indeed terrified by the collision scene. While others at the scene were rendering help, Freddie left the scene and drove home.

I thoroughly prepared Freddie for the witness stand before trial. I deliberately did not explore his reason for leaving the scene, or what he had done while gone, during direct examination. I felt his story would have more impact if this part came out on cross examination. When, at last, this crucial question was asked on cross, Freddie was ready.

With great sincerity Freddie admitted that he had been deeply shaken at the scene and had lost his head. All he could think of was to return to his new bride, a quarter of a mile away, and tell her what happened. The two of them then immediately knelt down by their bedside and prayed. Calmed and strengthened, Freddie returned to the scene accompanied by his bride.

151

There he reported a frank account of what had happened to the police. Freddie, whose car had not been touched by either colliding car, was not charged.

Freddie and his wife were the souls of honesty and remorse by admitting his horror and fright and his leaving the scene.

The twelve-person jury exonerated Freddie and rendered a verdict solely against the drinking, speeding sailor, home on leave.

Freddie and his wife, and their families, have remained my good friends through the years. Freddie and his wife and their families remain humble, God-fearing citizens to this day.

Miss Mary remained a member of my Sunday School class after her long recovery and despite crippling and disfigurement. After her death, I was consulted on matters relating to her estate by her brother, who lived in Norfolk, Virginia.

In our countryside, the lawyers know both sides of a lawsuit and, in order to make their living, often defend against friends who do not choose them to prosecute their sides of the case.

Another Case Among Friends

Another similar instance of opposing old family friends in court occurred near the end of my practice at the defense side of the table of the bar.

I was employed to defend Hollis Caldwell, who owned a few acres of land in the county along the highway north of Athens. He made his living cutting and hauling mine timbers to prop up the mine roofs in the coalfields. Hollis and his wife raised a nice family of three girls. They kept their small home and gardens along the highway in immaculate condition.

Very well known and respected Tom Weatherford, who was a retired cabinet and coffin maker in this same community, had raised a respectable and successful family. One of his boys, Brown Weatherford, was my age and we had known each other virtually all of our lives. Brown was married to a most popular school teacher, Margaret Mayberry. Her father was the widely-known and loved Methodist circuit riding preacher, just as my grandfather had been.

Old Tom Weatherford had a flat tire one evening while driving along the straight, level country road after dark. He stopped partly on and partly off the pavement. This was right in the mouth of a level, private, graveled driveway, where he could have easily got his car all of the way off the road. He was trying to change his rear tire with a jack sitting on the pavement. His battery must have been weak and he was using matches to help him see what he was doing.

At that point, Hollis Caldwell came along on his way home from delivering his props to the mine. He was almost home. The metal collar of Hollis' flatbed truck struck Mr. Weatherford. The result was massive external and internal injuries described by his experienced and popular local physician, Dr. Holroyd, as the worst injuries he had ever seen suffered by a person who survived. The hospital bills were immense.

The Weatherford family chose to employ the same highly touted, loud, "big gun" plaintiffs lawyer. He wanted to score a big verdict in this case between well-known citizens.

Hollis and his wife, Choline, made excellent, honest and contrite witnesses. The first trial of the case resulted in a hung jury. The second trial resulted in a plaintiffs verdict of a mere $1,500 award for the plaintiff. The Caldwell's home was saved. They had no insurance and, in fact, were defending their small homestead. The Caldwell family and their many neighbors remained my strongest friends over the years.

My old friend, Brown Weatherford, didn't speak to me for many years following the accident and his father's death, which occurred a very few years later. Finally, Brown has renewed our friendship. His fine wife taught our four children in public schools. This teacher's brother, Jimmy Mayberry, remains an excellent friend and the family have recommended other persons to me for legal services. I later consulted Jimmy and Margaret's mother when she was in a car accident in Virginia, after her husband, the preacher, had died. Preacher Mayberry, largely called Brother Mayberry, had a record of preaching more countryside funerals of his farming friends and parishioners than all of the other small country preachers combined. The Weatherford family is one of the oldest and respected countryside families. They elected their lawyer who wanted to make a notorious case, instead of trying to negotiate a settlement commensurate with the economic worth of the defendants, the Caldwells, who deserved a defense to such an onslaught. I gave it to them.

CIVIL RIGHTS

CROSSROADS OF LIFE
AND PRACTICE

Civil Rights Skirmish
on the Local Scene

Charlie Justice was the teacher of the largest Sunday School class in Princeton. The Men's Bible Class of the First Methodist Church had a membership of about 150 men, mostly railway employees. Mr. Justice had taught me in junior high school. He had seen me prosecute, before the school board of which he was a member, a male teacher who made advances toward young girls in his gym classes. I obtained that teacher's dismissal.

Mr. Justice *willed* me his Sunday school class before his death. He told the men that when he passed away he hoped they would ask me to be their teacher. I was teaching a women's class when a delegation from this class came to recruit me.

I took this teaching responsibility very seriously. Every Saturday night I would spend several hours at my desk in the library, writing out my lesson in long hand on yellow legal sheets. I taught the mens' class from 1957 to 1968.

These were the Civil Rights years. The issue confronted the nation, just as war and reconstruction had challenged us earlier. It was not a time to stand idly by. Everything I was studying and teaching told me to speak out.

As a teacher, I had official lesson material supplied me by the Methodist church. This literature, and the ancient Biblical passages I read to prepare my lessons, set forth the clear message of the brotherhood of man. As the old Methodist hymn proclaimed lustily, "There is no east nor west, no north nor south, but one great fellowship throughout the whole wide earth!". We Methodists, Baptists and all the rest could no longer sit in our segregated churches and simply preach and sing about the matter. We were involved.

The action moved right in among us and challenged our consciences throughout the countryside. People were speaking out. The ranks were divided, the sheep and the goats were being separated. One was either for or against the principles of Civil Rights and equal justice. I had fought for a better world and an equal society. Were we really the land of the free and the home of the brave?

The privilege of having a profession, a good home, four healthy children and a beautiful wife holding it all together was no longer to be taken for granted. My choice was clear. I had to cast my lot with those working for integration of the social order. This was a crossroads time in American history.

Across the nation, cities and towns were erupting in racial violence. Society was becoming polarized. This intense struggle played itself out in communities large and small. The old forms were being challenged and were dying hard. Those who resisted integration hated and feared the changes that were coming. Tension was building.

In the south, segregation had been pervasive. In our area, "Whites Only" signs were a common sight. At that time, a black man serving on a jury couldn't get his noon meal at any local restaurant unless he went to the back door. Therefore, a black juror had to either bring his lunch or go out of town to some remote black-run establishment and try his best to get back to court in time for the afternoon session.

Aerial showing the two Bluefields, separated by Hog Back Ridge, with the railway and the colored concentration and State college in the old original valley.

Focus On Bluefield

The Civil Rights movement caused alarm and paranoia among the white "power structure" in Bluefield, the radio, television, newspaper monopoly. Bluefield became the local proving ground of Civil Rights in southern West Virginia.

Bluefield was born in 1890 as the eastern coal shipping yard of the New N&W Railway. The town grew up rapidly in the narrow valley on both sides of the railway. The black population settled and congregated along the rail yard. This community became home to a black college, Bluefield Colored Institute now Bluefield State College, and became the cultural center for the large black population of the nearby Pocahontas coalfields.

The white gentry gradually deserted the original Victorian homes along the railway, in favor of the wider valley along East River Mountain. The parallel valleys were separated by a hog-backed ridge. White churches, banks and the business community remained along the railway. Meanwhile, the black community grew along the hillsides and ridge of the original town.

159

The Council on Human Relations

A Christian leadership organization, based in Atlanta, grew up with local chapters all through the south. A local chapter was formed, the Mercer-Tazewell Council on Human Relations. The membership included virtually all of the areas leading black preachers and many professors from Bluefield State College. Bluefield State president, Dr. Leroy Allen, and his highly educated wife, were active members, as was Carrolton Jackson, a bright young professor.

The Reverend N.W. Looney, pastor of Bluefield's Grace Methodist Church, a descendant of one of the oldest Methodist families in southwest Virginia, was the first president. He started writing letters to the Bluefield daily newspaper editor and building his membership.

Reverend Looney recruited me when I called to congratulate him on his excellent "Letter to the Editor." No other lawyer, doctor or business leader would come forward, except my old school friend from childhood days, Wilson Carter. Wilson owned the area's best mens' clothing store. I served two years as president and was succeeded by Wilson Carter.

Dr. Joseph Marsh, president of nearby Concord College, gave the organization his blessing. His Dean of Women, a Pennsylvania Quaker, Damaris Wilson, became a leading member of the organization and served as its president after Wilson Carter.

Pennsylvanian, Bill Berry, manager of Penney's Department Store in Bluefield was a strong early member. Bluefield Episcopal priest, Rev. Frank Rowley, a New Englander, also joined.

One of my best and oldest black friends was tall, straight, Joe Adams. He was chief hospital orderly in Princeton and was a person of great substance. Joe had been at the bedside when my sister Sarah died, when my father died, and when my grandfather died. Joe had been a comfort to sick people in the local hospital for fifty years. He and his wife and his sister-in-law, joined our organization.

Bridges of Understanding

Meeting together, discussing issues, was a revelation to both whites and blacks. We saw how alike we were. Our separate but "equal" schools, churches, social clubs and orders, had denied us the privilege of really knowing each other. Now we became friends in common cause. We saw each other as human beings, whose only difference was our color. By becoming well acquainted with each other, coloring became irrelevant. The colored leaders were every bit as cultivated or civilized as the whites. However, they were treated as distinctly second-class citizens. Our part of civil rights movement in the Human Relations Council was to create bridges of understanding and communication, to overcome the bigotry and ignorance.

The women members were especially effective. Damaris Wilson and other professional women, church and club leaders, would go around the community as a mixed group. They would get all dressed up, and go together to restaurants which displayed the "White Only" signs. The white restaurant owners thought we were trying to destroy their business. All our names were mud in the community.

The men in my Bible class knew me better than others and, though they were not participants in Civil Rights, they respected me. One of my best friends in the class, a family friend and an old line Methodist, was Early Robertson. Early was a machinist at the local railway shop, a Bible class member and a member of the church choir. When the Civil Rights issue arose in Bible class, he would ask the question aloud, "What are you going to say when the blacks and whites start marrying, and when your daughter dates a black man?"

Daughter Mary Takes a Stand

Our second child, Mary, now a leading trial attorney in the state capitol, was in high school when the Civil Rights issues were most intense. She belonged to a social club composed of girls from the homes of the town's gentry. She also wrote for the school newspaper. In that paper, Mary challenged her graduating class's policy of not permitting black classmates to attend the prom. The newly-formed West Virginia Human Commission sent an investigator down from the capitol to look into the matter. This caused a considerable alarm with the principal and school officials. A veritable tidal wave erupted.

Mary had spoken out. As a result she caught all kinds of pressure and negative reactions from her peers. The teacher sponsor of the girls' club strongly dissapproved; the same teacher who had told us Mary was a very promising and "creative" writer. When Mary's creativity crossed the color line the teacher/sponsor became sour. A menacing gang of students would wait for Mary after school, threatening harm to her. Katherine would pick-up Mary right after school and bring her home. It wasn't safe for her to ride the school bus. In spite of all of this Mary plowed right ahead with her crusade.

The high school and "colored hill" were close by each other on the west side of town. The segregated prom was held, not in the school gym, but off the school campus, at a private club on the east edge of town. Mary attended the prom with her date from across the state line in Virginia.

Late in the evening, I received a telephone call from the high school coach chaperoning the prom. He told me I had better come, that Mary was sick in the girls' bathroom. I went straight to the prom. I walked through the silent crowd to the girls' rest room. The coach and other chaperons were coolly aloof. I picked my unconscious daughter up from the floor and carried her, with her date following, back through the crowd in the dance hall to my car. I drove her to our home in the country, south of town.

I placed Mary on the bed in my mother's downstairs bedroom and called our old friend and doctor, Daniel Hale. He got out of bed and came right away. He examined Mary as she lay there, pulling open an eyelid. He said, "She's had a *Mickey-Finn,* but she'll be okay in a few minutes." I walked out of the front door into the yard with the doctor. While we were talking, Mary walked out of the house with her date. She said she was going back to the dance. I prohibited her from returning.

Radicals Bomb College

The efforts of our Human Relations Council had largely preempted the more militant elements. Militants were strong on the Bluefield State campus. The mens' and womens' dormitories each housed students from northern cities. They would come to our meetings and urge radical and provocative action. We listened and then pursued our steady course of integration through example, dialogue and economic pressure.

Finally, however, it happened. Bluefield State's mens' dormitory was bombed. This gave the "power structure" the cause they needed with state government. The "undersirables" could now be moved against. As a result of the bombing, both dormitories were closed permanently.

Bluefield State's President, Dr. Allen and Concord President, Dr. Marsh, were each transferred from the area. Under the guise of combining the administrations, a new president, named Coffindafer, was imported from the northern part of the state. He was given the impossible job of presiding over both colleges.

Concord College, in Athens, at the northern end of the county, had a small minority black student body, while Bluefield State, twenty miles away on the Virginia border, was mostly black. Princeton, with its small, non-political black population, lay between. This new white president, struggled with joint administration for two years.

When all the smoke cleared, Bluefield State became a predominantly white commuter college. The colleges reverted to separate administrations and presidents as before. This cleansing was orchestrated by the financial and banking power structure in Bluefield.

We Paid a Price

Everyone involved in our organization experienced discord in life and personal family relations. Black members caught static from the black community for allying with whites. White members reaped even more intense static from friends, churches, clubs and relatives. A rumor became widespread that I was employed by the National Association for the Advancement of Colored People, such organization being regarded as on a par with communism. My family would receive ugly, anonymous phone calls at night spewing hatred and threats.

All of us who had worked for change paid dearly. White minister, Reverend Looney, was transferred to rural, sleepy Alderson, in Greenbrier County. The black population there was practically nil. His health failed rapidly. He developed leukemia.

He had a beautiful wife and two fine sons, who were physicians, trained at Johns Hopkins University in Baltimore. One of them taught emergency room medicine and acupuncture at California School of Medicine at Berkeley. He often flew here, helping to prolong his father's life seven years by acupuncture treatments. I greatly admired this noble son.

Wilson Carter and Damaris Wilson each lived with the tremendous stress brought on by the the times and the positions our group took. They each experienced reverses and tragedies in their lives and families.

I paid my penalty in court. My stock with juries plummeted. All the good will I had inherited through my father and mother in the community seemed gone. Some of my "worthy adversaries" in court trials would, in picking juries, ask the prospective jurors if any were members of any "associations or organizations" that I belonged to, a veiled reference to my Civil Rights activities. My previously-charmed relationship with Mercer County juries plummeted.

All this negative reaction to me and my family by a twin turn of fate led me to greatly enlarge my law practice into the surrounding counties and away from the courts and juries of Mercer County.

THE HAND
OF
KIND
PROVIDENCE
CONTINUED

Crossroads of Fate – Practice Expands

Just as my local practice began to suffer, Kind Providence sent me the case of a lifetime. What follows is the central story of my career as a country lawyer.

During the hullabaloo surrounding my involvement with Civil Rights in 1960s, the God of fate and justice sent me the most important client of my entire years of law practice. Damon Williams, of the neighboring county of Summers, walked into my office totally unaware of our local Civil Rights tempest.

He told me that Nationwide Automobile Insurance Company had offered him a $20,000 settlement for his automobile accident injuries sustained near Danville, Virginia, in Pittsylvania County. He said that at least two named well-known leading plaintiff's lawyers of Mercer and Raleigh counties had been calling him and offering to take his case. He asked me how I was willing to handle his case. I offered to represent him for one-third contingent fee over and above the first $20,000. He accepted my contract and told me the reason he came to see me was because I taught the Mens' Bible Class and his friends had told him about me in this connection. A vital part of the plaintiff's contingency fee practice is the ability to evaluate cases. Having served the defense, I knew both sides and knew the value of my cases by close association with my clients.

Damon was an outstandingly popular automobile dealer, full of personality and drive. He had won first prize for twenty-five straight years for Ford cars sold in the several state Cincinnati District. An official from the Cincinnati home office so testified. Damon's amazing sales record was even more amazing when you realize it was performed at a dealership in Hinton, West Virginia, in rural Summers County. Damon sold cars in a fifty-mile radius including the counties of Summers, Monroe, Greenbrier, Raleigh and Mercer. Damon was well-known in these surrounding counties.

He and I had formed a terrific lawyer/client bond. He let the public know of his faith in me. This one case, and one client, changed my practice from a primarily defense practice to an exclusively plaintiff's practice.

Damon had a keen sense of humor. He could play five musical instruments at a time. He often did so at the annual Coon Hunters Banquet in Summers County. When this came out at trial the fact was reported in the *New York Times*. The opposition tried to ridicule Damon for this but that worked against them. We must have had some coon hunters on the jury.

While in the hospital he had used his ability as a ventriloquist to fool nurses into believing he had all sorts of strange bodily problems. In reality his accident had left him with a serious knee injury requiring a permanent, and restrictive, knee brace. This greatly constricted his activities and his, previously very dynamic, life-style. This was a strong case and he was a highly effective witness.

The case was tried in Federal Court in Danville. The insurance coverage limit was $100,000. In the 1960s that was an awful lot of money. At the start of the trial, the insurance company offered to settle for $40,000. I had hired my law school friend, Jimmy Edmunds, of neighboring Halifax County, Virginia, to assist as local counsel. Jim nearly fell out with me when I declined this offer. But he didn't know the amount of preparation I had in the case. He just couldn't appreciate the value of the case as I could from my close association and identification with this most intelligent and appealing client.

One of the jurors there in Danville was a fine-looking lady, the wife of a surgeon. Her husband had learned his orthopedic surgery at the University of Virginia, under my star medical witness, Dr. Hamilton Allen, chief of the Department of Orthopedic Surgery. I could tell that defense lawyers from Danville felt confident this lady was their friend.

I elected to bring Dr. Hamilton Allen to personally testify at the trial. I left the local West Virginia "bone doctor" at home, simply reading his cold deposition, wherein he gave the opinion that the brace might be removed after a reasonable time. I had engaged Dr. Allen for a second opinion and he strongly testified the brace had to be worn for life. Needless to say he was well received by the jury.

Even though my co-counsel didn't like it, Damon had stuck with my recommendation not to settle. The jury gave us $90,000 plus costs of over $700.

It's hard to appreciate here in the 1990s how sensational that verdict was received in the general community at the time in the 1960s. When the jury verdict was received in the courtroom, the judge, Ted Dalton, a former trial lawyer who had personally represented Nationwide Insurance Company, called the lawyers into his chambers and told the defense counsel, "You've been damn fools not to have settled this case and any appeal will be useless."

We'd had numerous pretrial conferences in which we had fully disclosed settlement negotiations to the judge. The chief insurance adjuster from Lynchburg had attended the conferences, including one the day before the trial, when the $40,000 offer was made. The judge had personally called the chief adjuster from Lynchburg to that conference, having represented that insurance company and that chief claim adjuster before he became judge.

A law school classmate, practicing in Danville, Virginia, told me after the trial that our verdict was about twice as high as any former personal injury verdict ever returned in that courthouse. I received a $15,000 whiplash verdict the same week, tried on a Thursday and Friday before the same judge sitting in the Roanoke Federal Courthouse. Judge Dalton told me jokingly to get out of Virginia, that he didn't want to see me for a long time.

I Hit the Road

The trial for this very popular citizen, Damon Williams, put me on the map and on the road. Damon's wide circle of friends became my circle of friends and clients. By virtue of this singular case, I was able to establish an exclusive plaintiffs practice in a wide area.

I became less dependent on my local county juries, which were prejudiced against me for my Civil Rights activities. In a small town, your friends can be your worst enemies, especially if you have turned them out of your office and they have set up their own competing practice. The success of Damon Williams' case proved to be the vehicle by which I was able to get out of my hometown. I got on the road, winning friends and cases abroad, making a regional name for myself in the practice of law.

At the time, there was a popular western cowboy television serial program entitled, "Have Gun, Will Travel." My practice became, "Have Briefcase, Will Travel." I carried large bulky briefcases to my trials, "loaded for bear." I also used all the modern demonstrative devices, pictures, models, charts, etc., to glamorize my cases. I received notably large verdicts.

Country Juries, Small Verdicts

Despite Damon Williams' popularity and the fame of his case, Summers, Greenbrier and Monroe County juries were in the habit of small verdicts. No one wanted his neighbor to have more than he had. Auto insurance adjusters thought they were doing great charity to simply pay the hospital bills of injured parties and get full release of their claims. Therefore, the insurance companies in these three counties valued injury claims extremely low. Lawyers from the large cities refused to take cases in those counties because of the notoriously low verdicts rendered by the local juries.

It was hard to break this pattern. I obtained good verdicts and recoveries when I could bring suits involving their citizens in other counties, as when the injuries occurred elsewhere such as in neighboring Raleigh County where verdicts were valued higher.

I obtained substantial awards for Summers County residents in Railway employee cases. This was by bringing the cases to trial elsewhere, in more metropolitan areas. By law the Railway could be sued in any jurisdiction where they did business, all up and down the line. Several of my railroad injury cases were brought in Roanoke and tried in the Federal District Court there. These juries placed a higher value on suffering and disability.

Elk Knob Clientele

The highest peak in Summers County is Elk Knob of Keeney's Mountain. The leading citizen of this remote and scenic country is big Marion O'Bryan, large general storekeeper at the crossroads of Hix in this high country and who also served as court deputy sheriff and bailiff for a large part of my practice years in Summers County. During this time, Judge Nickel Kramer, who never owned a car and didn't drive, presided over the four counties of Summers, Greenbrier, Monroe and Pocahontas, a vast territory of four courthouses.

Probably on the recommendation of my friend, Deputy

O'Bryan, I represented a handsome young citizen of Elk Knob who became a city policeman of the county seat of Hinton. This young man who had a nice wife and several kids, had a car wreck on a one-lane road (of which there are many in the remote areas of both Summers and Mercer County.) It was a pure question of who was "hogging" the one-lane narrow road on the crest of a hill.

My star witness was a very pretty, tall, red-haired teenage girl who lived beside the road at the collision site and who was an eye-witness. She made a very effective witness. We won a very nice verdict and recovery in the Summers County Court. My client's injury was a crippled right hand, with permanent nerve injury in the wrist area. He was disabled as a policeman.

He had a very sufficient secondhand car and promised me he would use his handsome recovery wisely. As soon as the money recovery was in his pocket, he traded his secondhand car for a new car and bought an old grocery store near the courthouse in downtown Hinton – store building, stock in trade and all the charge accounts of the customers. He bought this bonanza of trouble from Constable Acel Pettry. In a very short time, he was broke with the charge-account grocery store.

The redhaired star witness asked me to be "best man" at her wedding with an older man she met soon after the trial. Katherine and I attended the wedding in the home on Beach Run outside Hinton. At the conclusion of the wedding, the bride and groom went to a funeral wake, while Katherine and I returned to our home twenty-seven miles away.

Local Law Enforcement

Constable Acel Pettry of an old Summers/Mercer County family, was a small man, always in his black uniform and hat, with weapon and his billy club strapped on his side. Shortly after the young policeman's trial in Hinton, Acel had gone to the home of two or three unmarried brothers located high on the bank of Beach Run outside of Hinton to quell a disturbance. Some neighbors had complained the boys were too loud and were disturbing the neighborhood. Acel proceeded as a one man army into the house where the brothers had been drinking for several days anything they could find of an alcoholic nature. He proceeded to beat up on the old boys with his nightstick. They came to see me about their injuries. I sued Acel on his policeman's bond and recovered more money than the old boys knew how to spend, unless it was to buy a little better brand of whiskey – and life went on, a little more subdued than before.

Contract of Employment

My father had taught me always to have a written contract of employment at the outset of my representation of a client.

One of the best old Hinton area families had a fine son about to enter veterinary school in Ohio. In the summer of his final college year at West Virginia University prior to veterinary schooling, he dated a certain pleasingly-plump neighbor girl who also had several other suitors. The young lady got pregnant. She charged the promising young son of the prominent family as the father of her illegitimate son.

I met with the family. They signed my written contract, wherein I agreed to represent the boy for a set fee of $500. I failed to provide any contingencies for any retrial or appeal.

The first two jury trials resulted in hung juries. At the third trial, I got the boy off and he went away to veterinary school and to another state and did well. I earned a great lot of goodwill, while nearly bankrupting my law office in the long, drawn-out process.

Thus, I became the new lawyer in Summers County, over a period of years, where trials for negligent injury – torts – were not the rule. The local lawyers were an honorable, easy-going lot, but didn't get out of their offices to investigate cases. Tom Reed, prosecuting attorney, was the acknowledged best fisherman in the county where the three major rivers, the New River, Bluestone River and Greenbrier River, all converged. He had quite an assortment of lures in his desk drawer in his court-house office, where he sat with his peg leg propped up in his oversized swivel chair, with a desk drawer out working on an assortment of lures.

Bill Brown, Fred Sawyers, Jess Wise, Perry Mann and Colonel Harold Eagle were the rest of the Summers County Bar in my heyday at the Summers County Courthouse. Fred Saw-yers was well fixed and ran a couple of family coal mines down the river from Hinton. His practice was mostly land titles and banking. Jess was divorce commissioner and commissioner of

estate accounts. Bill Brown was an easy going, gentleman lawyer. His brother, Perry, was Federal District Attorney. Bill's son,
James, is now one of the leading trial lawyers in Beckley. Harold
Eagle was in trials all of the time, mostly criminal. I tried many
cases with Harold, while the other lawyers were content without jury trials. Harold's father and my father were old Republican friends and political war horses. Harold served as mayor of
the town frequently. He taught the mens' Bible class of the

Summers County victorian courthouse at Hinton.

Hinton Methodist Church. I taught the mens' Bible class at the
Princeton Methodist Church. Harold was one of the last of the
old Bible-quoting lawyers of the old school. He would quote the
Bible in his court arguments and I would counterquote the Bible
in our skirmishes in the old Victorian Courthouse where the
bell in the tower regularly announced the opening of court.

I became a regular member of the Summers County Bar
and paid my dues for a number of years. Summers County citizens would often drive twenty-seven miles between Hinton and
Princeton courthouses and drop by my office to engage me in
their grievances – without calling in advance for an appointment – just as they had always done in the easy-going town of
Hinton. That is the reason I didn't open an office at Hinton, as

173

Hinton news editor John Faulkner, urged me to do – because of
the custom of dropping in lawyer's offices. When they drove
twenty-seven miles, they usually had something worth looking
into, even though they didn't call ahead.

The City Dump Case

The city of Hinton, in Summers County, dumped the town's
garbage high on the side of a hill in the low-income west end of
town. It was smelly and unsightly and caused rats to run all
over the nieghborhood. The city had created an eyesore, a nui-
sance, and, as it turned out, a disaster in the making.

The garbage had a habit of stopping up the creek bed in the
valley below the dump. The health officer, venerable and most
popular Dr. J.D. Stokes, had repeatedly warned the town council of the problems and had suggested a culvert to prevent the
stoppage of the creek.

One night, during a heavy rainfall, a great portion of the
dump sheared off the mountainside, dammed up the creek and
caused a lake of water to form. The pressure from all this water
built-up and pushed an island of garbage down the valley, over
and through my several clients' homes.

We brought these cases on for trial before a jury in the Summers County Circuit Court right there in Hinton. The city's defense was that the disaster was an "act of God." The jury thought
otherwise and found the city liable for damages. We were
awarded the value of these destroyed houses.

The city appealed to the Supreme Court on their theory. The
Supreme Court upheld our judgment saying that God was not
solely to blame for the situation since he had gotten so much
assistance from the city fathers. The city of Hinton had no money
and had to raise taxes on the electric power company and other
utilities to pay off the large verdicts.

This case gave a lot of hope to the citizenry and increased
the size of verdicts in that community. Much of the credit belonged to courageous Dr. Stokes. This same Dr. Stokes later sent
me a case against a certain knife-happy surgeon who caused a
Beckley pathologist to remark that he never saw as many healthy
gall bladders to compare to those sent to him by this particular
surgeon.

The Drag Race Case

Another case that elevated the thinking of the Summers County jurors was the notorious drag race case.

Two carloads of young men, sons of leading Hinton citizens, decided one night to have a drag race at the three-quarter mile straight and level Route Three, along the Greenbrier River at the edge of town. The cars started out near the armory at the beginning of the straightway and, as they ended the race three-quarter miles along the straight course, the lead car slowed down and the loser zoomed past the winner, just as my client, welfare recipient Calvin Adkins, with his wife and young daughter in his pickup truck, appeared around the curve. A terrible crash occurred, killing Calvin's wife and his young daughter.

The insurance paid the maximum statutory amount for the life of the daughter, but I had to bring suit to obtain a suitable award for the life of the mother. This trial established a state-wide precedent.

The "Wrongful Death" statute in West Virginia, at that time, limited death recovery to $10,000, plus any provable economic loss up to a total of $25,000. Our jury verdict of $23,500 was based on proof of economic value of services of a housewife not otherwise gainfully employed. This concept had never been established in the courts of the state before this trial.

Our star witness was a very attractive native daughter named Miss Louise Spangler. She had just retired and returned to her old family farm home in Summers County overlooking Bluestone River. Her career had been as a Chief Administrator at the Social Security headquarters in Washington, DC. I qualified her as an expert witness to translate into monetary terms the market value of a homemaker's services, such as cooking, sewing, canning, gardening and making a home for her husband and children. The conservative jurors, still not thoroughly convinced that some insurance company would foot the bill, and fearing that some of these leading families might have to contribute, didn't give the full $25,000. However, their verdict was considered sensational in that community at that time.

This was part of the painfully slow evolution of tort law from the dark ages of the English common law where a pedigreed bull or blooded race horse had no limit of recovery, while human life was limited by the ancient English Lord Campbell's Act. This outdated law was in effect in our courts until recent years.

Spinoff Cases:
The Stolen Farm and Other Cases

The older I became, and the more experienced in the practice, the more willing I was to take the hard case. And the more willing to be sympathetic with the hard luck story of the client who couldn't find anyone else to take his case. Two such cases, from the Summers County area, were spinoffs from the Damon Williams case.

One of these cases involved the recently-widowed Polly. She came looking for me one day when I was out of the office. She had driven over from the beautiful high farming country of Monroe County, two counties away. She had been sent to see me by her next farm neighbor, my friend, Hamilton Sharp, a land surveyor, who was also senior warden in the Episcopal Church in Hinton, West Virginia.

She talked to my son Henry and told her case to him. He told her he would talk to me and see if we could take the case. We discussed her case around the office. The other lawyers all felt that this was a most improbable case and an absolute loser. I, however, told them I was convinced of the truth of her case. This was because I knew the background of the person she wanted to sue.

Polly and her husband owned a seven hundred-acre dairy farm in Monroe County, just across the border from Summers County. Her husband was the bookkeeper and the brains behind that operation. He was an old broken-down World War II veteran with a heart condition. At the time Polly had been just a teenage girl.

Polly was pure country, a bumptious, outgoing and very able-bodied farm girl. She took care of all the rough chores on the farm, including fencing and rounding up the herds for the milking process. She was the classic cowgirl and wore her riding jeans well. She enjoyed farming tremendously but knew nothing whatsoever about the business end of it all.

The farm belonged to her husband's parents. After her father-in-law died the farm was about to go under. The family got together and decided to get a Farmer's Home, low (five percent) interest loan to keep the farm place operating as a dairy. They put it all in the name of Polly and her husband jointly.

The couple ran the farm for many years as a profitable venture, largely because of Polly's hard work. Her husband had two brothers who had nothing to do with the running of the farm. One of those brothers was a gambler, a tavern keeper and a thorough going rascal. He lived twenty miles away in the town of Hinton, the county seat of nearby Summers County.

When Polly's husband died, he willed his half interest to his wife and made her the executrix in his will. She had no ability or competence to administer the estate and, therefore, asked her brother-in-law in Hinton to do the job for her. And so he did, with a vengeance. He proceeded to take the farm from her by transfer deeds and out conveyances to himself and others.

Now it's hard to understand how anybody could steal a farm. However I was convinced that this very guileless female had been the victim of subterfuge and cunning. This is because I knew her rascally brother-in-law from a prior case.

I had previously represented a railroad engineer in Summers County, a decent man, in a contested divorce case. In that case this gambler brother-in-law had fiddled around with my client's wife. I proved adultery against his wife. In that divorce case, the wife had warned my witnesses that they would rue the day they testified against her. Shortly after divorce hearings, which we won, two of our witnesses lost their homes to fires clandestinely set in the night. I also knew that the wife's paramour had collected insurance from some of his own rental properties after they were burned. In fact, one of these fires occurred when he was in California with my client's wife. He had some cronies to do his dirty work.

In the farm stealing case, I had to prove that my client, the widow, was dumb enough to become the victim of such obvious fraud. It took a lot of woodshedding. She came across very convincingly at the trial. The jury set aside the transactions and restored the title to my client. The judge sustained that verdict and on the appeal to the Supreme Court we were again sustained.

Notwithstanding our victory, Polly was so inept in business that she was not able to resume operation of the farm. She sold

out, married a retired coal miner and moved with him to Mc-
Dowell County, several counties away.

Death Case of an
Eighteen-Year-Old Son

Another spinoff case from Summers County was the acci-
dental automobile death case of Rex Garten of Summers County.
He died on his eighteenth birthday. Rex and his father had become at odds with each other during the teenage identity crisis
of this only son.

The boy was celebrating his birthday alone in the evening
at a nearby tavern by the bank of the Greenbrier River along
Route Three. The young man had consumed a number of "red
eyes," a drink which is some kind of combination of liquor and
beer. He became highly intoxicated.

During that same evening two young salesmen came into
the tavern and were drinking alcoholic beverages when their
wives, and one or more the their infant children, came into the
tavern. They shamed their husbands for deserting them. The
two men exchanged vehicles with their wives. They gave their
wives the pickup truck they had arrived in and took the wives'
new car. This scene publicly humiliated the two salesmen. They
immediately departed the tavern for home.

Rex Garten also left the tavern, alone. He got in his car,
drove up the slight incline of the graveled parking lot and onto
Highway Three. Spinning his wheels going out of the parking
lot, gravel was thrown against the salesmens' new vehicle. He
proceeded toward Hinton, which was in the opposite direction
of his father's home. The men followed Rex onto the highway
and continued to follow his car at an extremely high rate of speed.
When they came to the straightway, known locally as "the drag
strip," near the armory, these boys bumped the rear of Rex's car.
This sent it into a tailspin, throwing Rex out of his car and into
the middle of the road. Rex was hit by the front grill of the pursuing vehicle. He was killed instantly. The salesmen kept going
down the road. They returned after a short time.

The state police reported that the accident was due solely to
highly inebriated state of the deceased. They based this on the
blood tests. The Garten family was greatly humiliated, person-

ally and in the eyes of their community. The father, Leonard, was greatly distraught when he came to my office. My partner Lane Austin and I took on his case to prove the whole story of causation in this tragic accident.

From the beginning, we involved the father very heavily in our investigations. This gave him a reason for living. We engaged an accident reconstruction expert from Cary, North Carolina. We also took discovery depositions of the salesmen. We freely and preemptively admitted the highly intoxicated state of our client's son. Nonetheless, we proved that he was the victim, rather than the perpetrator of this horrible automobile accident.

At the trial, the deceased's twin sister and his older sister were so embarrassed that they refused to come to court. I had to apply great persuasion to get them to come to the courtroom and participate in the trial. They finally agreed to do so. During the long pendency of the case, Mrs. Garten was the moral force keeping the family spirits together. After the trial, and the hung jury that resulted, the insurance company made a reasonable compromise offer and the case was settled.

The family felt vindicated and had a virtual new birth.

Regina, Rex's twin, went to Bluefield State College and got her degree in Criminal Justice. She is now married and works for an automobile liability insurance company out of St. Albans, West Virginia. She has a six-year-old son named Rexford, after her lost twin brother. This grandson is a great source of pride and pleasure to the Gartens.

The older daughter went to England and taught in an air force base school for three years. She has since obtained a masters degree and returned to her home area. She is presently employed as a school counselor in Fayette County.

After the father and the two sisters regained their stability, the mother went into a brief period of let down. She had carried the rest of the family through the long ordeal. Now, the whole family has gained a completely better perspective on life and the two sisters "can't do enough for others," the mother says. The father is now in retirement and they are all most respected citizens of their community. This is an example of a country practice of law, which is built on such client relationships that endure indefinitely.

Medical and Legal Negligence

I have tried a few malpractice cases against lawyers and a few malpractice cases against doctors. Most of those against doctors were referred to me by other doctors. I sued a Raleigh County lawyer from Beckley, who was popular with the local Bar Association and whose brother or uncle had been a state governor. Despite his illustrious family connections, he was a do-less lawyer. I won that case. Afterwards the Raleigh County lawyers quit speaking to me for about a year.

It is necessary, in order to win a case in medical or legal malpractice case, that you have at least one other doctor or lawyer willing to testify that the conduct of the defendant doctor or lawyer was contrary to accepted professional standards. This is required to support a claim of medical or legal negligence.

Death by Appendicitis Operation

One of our medical malpractice cases was against a Harvard-educated physician and surgeon who had caused the death of a twenty-five year old man. The doctor had operated upon him for appendicitis, a condition he did not have. The surgical intervention had produced an adynamic ileus, which simply means nonfunctional portion of the intestine from being handled during surgery. Neither the failure to diagnose that the appendix did not require operation nor the fact that the ileus was offended was a negligent act. These things are normal and routine and happen often.

The malpractice, or medical negligence, was the repeated failure of the doctor to alleviate the impaction resulting from the adynamic ileus. As a result the patient became highly constipated. After repeated warnings from the family and communications to the nurses, the doctor refused to attend the situation. Instead he attended a Christmas party. The patient died on his vomitus. Our expert in the case was head of the surgical department at the University of Pennsylvania. He testified that it is pretty hard to kill a twenty-five year old boy, but, because this doctor failed to adequately diagnose and treat the failure of intestinal tract function he was guilty of a high degree of medical negligence.

OTHER
MAJOR CASES
REMEMBERED

Playground Case

After Civil Rights in my town of Princeton, the all-black school in a separate colored section of the town called "The Hill" was converted by the board of education to a school for special (gifted or brighter than others) students. The school was brick and not too old to be put out of use when the black students were bussed to the former all-white schools.

The playground that surrounded the school building was newly-paved with asphalt after the changeover. In the center of the playground, on a slight slope, an old "monkey bar" was retained. It was a tall, awkard, homemade monstrosity leftover from the all-black school, unpaved dirt playground. The "Special Education" children of the fifth through seventh grades played on the bar during recess periods under supervision of alternating teachers.

Our client was a young couple whose very precocious and very healthy young son was showing off on the bar for other students. He fell off the bar and sustained a very serious head injury on the asphalt surface.

The school's insurance carrier denied liability, negligence or culpability. We filed suit and, under the terms of the insurance coverage, the school principal and teachers were "covered." We named the principal as defendant on the basis of agency and supervision of teachers on the playground and sued the board of education also for creating an inherently dangerous playground. We had a "mock-up" of the monkey bars by finding the old bars, which had been given away to serve as clothesline posts. We brought the exact replica into court.

The first trial resulted in a hung jury because we overlooked an insurance salesman in the jury selection process. The second trial brought a good verdict.

The principal, a middle-aged, dignified man of an excellent old family in the same church I attended, felt the whole thing was a personal affront to his character and reputation and a cool atmosphere prevailed in our church relations from then on. I have and still have high respect for the man and his family, but I did my duty as a plaintiff's lawyer in my small and intimate community.

Doctor Von Elbe and the Car Fire

I had already won a negligence case with very serious personal injury against General Motors for the failure of the brakes of a Corvair automobile when I was hired to prosecute a highly interesting case against the Ford Motor Company.

A young mother of two infant children had to pick up diapers that had just been laundered. She parked her new Ford automobile at the curb and turned the motor off. Since this would only take a few minutes, she left her two infant babes in the car's back seat as she went into a house. She returned to the car in five minutes. Within that time, the car had caught on fire. The heat was so intense that she couldn't pull open the door of the car. Her two babies were incinerated before her eyes.

At trial this horrible case turned out to be a battle of the experts. The stakes were very high. The trial was held before Judge Berkeley Lilly in Raleigh County. There had been a lot of tests and demonstrations performed by experts for each side. Our expert witness was Doctor Gunther Von Elbe. He had his early training at the University of Berlin, and spoke broken English with a heavy German accent.

Ford's defense was based on the theory that the mother had left a cigarette in the car and that it had caught the seat covers on fire and produced the quick fire.

Doctor Von Elbe was able to discover a very critical piece of evidence hidden in among the ashes and charred remains of the car. This was a small spring, not any larger than a pencil and about an inch long. Its condition after the fire was very critical evidence. This new Ford automobile, which had been driven less than six hundred miles, had been taken back to the dealer several times with smoke coming from the steering column. That is where all of the wires that controlled all of the various and sundry automatic devices on the car are located in a sheath. He proved that these wires had been shorted so many times that the wire covering had become hydrocarbon. This then ignited with explosive force and created an instant fire with the foam rubber in the car creating a tremendous, fast fire.

The opposition's expert did a demonstration of the same vintage automobile in North Carolina and had movies of their attempt to ignite the wire coverings by frequent electric shorts

184

offending the same. The critical difference was that our car had its wire covering gradually reduced to a highly-combustible state by numerous electrical shortages until this covering became an explosive.

The strange thing about that case was that, at the time we tried it, the life of a mere infant child babe in arms was only worth $10,000 under the ancient rule of the Lord's Campbell's act. Invented in England years ago this rule had not been changed at that time in America. Therefore, Ford was able to defend that case without danger of a high verdict.

Our expert stayed with the case because of his scientific curiosity. He was aware of similar complications in the same vintage motor vehicle and he wanted the reputation of disclosing this fault. Before the jury Dr. Von Elbe was captivating. He had complete mastery of his subject and communicated with warmth and humor. He is easily the best and most qualified expert I have ever seen in the courtroom.

Don Hodson, the capable attorney for Ford, probably received more money in his fee and cost than the total of our verdict of $10,000 for the life of each child. He had no duty to disclose his fee, but he did brag about getting a new car as a bonus. This fine lawyer of leading defense firm of File, Hudson and Payne, is a very decent and honorable man. He did his best and honest job for Ford Motor Company. Not long after this case was concluded over several years duration, Don Hodson quit the practice of law and went into the banking business. The delay in concluding this case allowed Ford Motors to get out of the limelight for building this particular vintage of Ford cars with overloaded electrical gadgets located in a column of wires up the steering column with a record of spontaneous fires, most of which did not result in death or injury.

In the first trial of the case, we had engaged an expert witness from the engineering department of West Virginia University. The man proved to be an expert on straddling the fence and obfuscating the issue. The result was a hung jury. The second trial, a year or so later, we found a real expert, German-born and educated Dr. Gunther Von Elbe. He proved our case by most skillful knowledge and experiments done first in the basement of our new law offices and then as demonstrations in the actual courtroom. Ford's expert said the fire must have been caused by the mother leaving her cigarette on the seat cover of the car.

Among other demonstrations in the courtroom, Dr. Von Elbe demonstrated the fallacy of this defense by leaving a lighted cigarette on the same brand of seat cover in front of the jury. After a long interval of several minutes, with the judge, jury and counsel, the judge said, "I think it has burned long enough."

Finally, after our trial, the infamous Lord Campbell's Act, inherited from England, has been repealed in American jurisprudence. The auto industry and their insurance compatriots are now mounting huge public compaigns to curtail the right of redress for product manufacture defects as "tort reform" to protect them from large verdicts; whereas, the Lord Campbell's Act was their license to kill in the older days.

A Cold Case

One medical negligence case against a hospital had an unusual aspect. I got the case about twenty years after the negligent act had occurred. Normally the statute of limitations requires a case to be brought within two years of the occurrence. However this does not begin to run until the negligent act is discoverable to a plaintiff.

In this case my client from Raleigh County, did a lot of golf playing. One of his buddies was a medical doctor. He had repeated sore throats over the years and kept complaining to this physician golf buddy. The doctor thought the frequency of this complaint was hard to explain. As a result he X-rayed the neck of my client and found a broken needle imbedded there. As it turned out the needle had migrated right next to his carotid artery. This was the cause of frequent sore throats which were otherwise unexplainable.

I was hard put to dig up evidence of how this needle got in his throat. He had his tonsils removed at a Bluefield hospital twenty years before. At that time he was a very young man and in the greatest good health. The evidence was pretty cold. Most of the doctors had departed the scene and the particular doctor who performed tonsilectomies had left the country. He had a well-known reputation for drinking. It was most likely he was fired from this hospital on account of his alcoholic habits.

One of the consulting doctors was still alive and confined to his home in a last, lingering illness. He had married his nurse, a much younger woman, and she was looking after him at home.

He had grown up in Pulaski, Virginia, and was a friend of an old family friend of mine who was an old-time lawyer of that community. Based on our mutual acquaintance, I was able to visit the sick doctor's home. He wanted to clear his conscience of this matter. He told me that he was present consulting when the surgeon broke the needle off. The tonsilectomy proceeded. After x-raying the broken needle in the throat, the team of doctors, including the hospital owner (since deceased), considered it was not in a dangerous, threatening position and decided not to tell the patient. They covered the matter up. I was able to dig out of the very old and musty records one little piece of evidence. It was a written report of an x-ray showing the fact that the needle was imbedded in the neck. These facts were proved by pretrial discovery depositions and procedures, and a most favorable settlement was obtained prior to trial.

RAILWAY
CASES

Buck Hatcher and the
Railway Case Runner

I have several times advised clients who came to see me and complained of having hired a lawyer who was not properly or adequately handling their case. A lot of people don't seem to understand they have a right to fire their lawyer. I have advised such clients to first get rid of the incompetent counsel and pay him what he charges for services to date before taking a written contract to further, and adequately, prosecute their case.

One such lawyer in a neighboring county had invited my prospective client into his office to meet with the insurance adjuster. The lawyer, client and adjuster all sat down in the same room and tried to settle the claim in a very friendly manner. The lawyer had not thoroughly investigated the seriousness of the man's injury in the first place. This lawyer, who would later become a judge, wasn't putting any effort into getting this client an adequate recovery for his serious injury. He wasn't much of a lawyer and he didn't become much of a judge. He should have been in a less combative occupation.

I sent the client back to his first lawyer and told him to ask the fellow what his services were worth and to tell him that he wanted to hire another lawyer. He paid the lawyer and came back to me. We got him a very nice recovery. We certainly didn't allow him to represent himself by talking to the adjusters. That was our job instead of the litigants.

Instead of suing incompetent lawyers, I did them a favor by getting the client to fire them before they damaged the client irrevocably and would have had to be sued for their wrong-doing.

Another such case of this order involved an old high school friend of mine, "Buck" (Justin Green) Hatcher, who worked in the local Princeton yard of the Virginian Railway. He was an electrician. He was required to climb a very ancient chestnut pole to take out of service a certain electric line. There was no obvious defect in this pole but it was rotted below ground and out of sight. When my friend cut the service off of the pole, it broke. My client fell all of the way to the ground holding to the pole. The pole fell partly on top of him, crushing him and causing numerous serious bodily injuries.

191

A "runner" from a Detroit law firm named Ryan said he had been informed of this accident through railroad union representatives. He came to my client's home in a big Cadillac. He promised him glowing recovery if he would hire a certain Detroit lawyer who was very skilled in railroad injuries. He took my client to Detroit in his Cadillac and went to the lawyer's office. My client signed a contract for a contingency fee of any recovery. He was then taken across the street to an orthopedic surgeon's office for examination. The physical report was to be sent back to the lawyer.

This Detroit lawyer had the case laying around his office, along with a multitude of other cases from all around the country, for about a year. When my client objected about the delay, the runner took the case to still another lawyer, this time, I believe, in Baltimore. That lawyer also handled a number of these choice cases, collected by Ryan over several states.

Another year went by, finally the Baltimore lawyer called my friend and client at his home and told him he had a $20,000 offer. He said he thought it was a good offer and that my client should take it.

My client was a little more intelligent than that. He came to see me. After we talked, I told him I thought the suggestion of $20,000 was a very small recovery considering the seriousness of his injuries and the nature of the accident. I even helped my old friend write a letter to the lawyer in the big city, firing the lawyer and asking him to submit a bill which, if it was within reason, would be paid out of any final recovery. Even then, I finally had to get on the phone and tell this big city character that my friend not only had the right to fire him, but also the right to sue him for malpractice.

I proceeded with Buck Hatcher's case. We took the case to trial in Charleston. We got a recovery from that jury that was many times the suggested recovery of the second lawyer. So much for big city lawyers and their professional runners.

I finally settled the other lawyer's "fee" after he filed Notice of a Lien against our recovery. However, I first made him do a little work to get the very small portion of that fee he was eventually paid.

We would have gotten an even larger verdict in this case had not the railroad offered a rebuttal witness in the form of the local yardmaster. He testified that the plaintiff was considered a very valuable employee. That the plaintiff had been kept on the job in light duty in order that his income should not be reduced by lost wages. He also stated that, after the trial, the railroad would keep the plaintiff on light duty until his retirement age. He stated the railroad would do this even though they knew the plaintiff was seriously and totally disabled.

This witness, who lived in our same town of Princeton, was told to testify to this falsehood. Just as soon as the recovery was paid out to my client, he was directed to go to Roanoke to the company doctor for a physical examination. As a result he was promptly disqualifed for further service and was retired. This railway yardmaster, who was well known to me in the community, and was in my church, never looked me in the face thereafter. I think he died a few years later with very diminished self-respect.

Buck Hatcher later told me that, upon his return from Roanoke and the examination, he confronted his neighbor, the yardmaster with the matter. The yardmaster had testified, "The way thing stand now, he can come back and do bench work and not have to do his regular job." After he was dismissed the yardmaster told Hatcher, "The claims department took it out of my hands." He added the doctor felt that Hatcher could not go back to work because of danger to other employees.

The railway, which by then had been bought by and consolidated with the larger Norfolk & Western, had required its yardmaster to testify to a falsehood and represent officially that its long-time employee would not be terminated. As I have found to be the case from my long experience, the larger the corporation, the more readily will its officer tell a lie to serve the money interest of the company. My client is a very rugged and a highly-respected native citizen. He is still alive, and will readily testify to the truth of this story about the railway officials fabrication of the truth.

The Case of Conductor Willey

A highly-respected Hinton citizen, seventy-one-year-old Arthur A. Willey, was still serving as train conductor on the C&O Railway when he was injured on the job in the Covington, Virginia, yard. He and his crew had alighted from their train at the end of their run, several tracks away from the railway station platform. This required them to traverse several intervening tracks to leave work. There was a regular raised platform across these several tracks for such movement of personnel in the yard. Conductor Willey and his crew walked along this pathway toward the station.

On one of the tracks which crossed this pathway, Pullman cars were being steamed. They were receiving steam in their pipes to get them ready to carry passengers to and from the Hot Springs Resort, located not far from Covington on a sideline from the main railway. There was a leak in the coupling where the steam was being transferred to the cars which sent up a cloud of steam right to the point of the normal personnel crossing where Mr. Willey and his crew were traversing. That cloud of steam blocked their vision as they crossed the tracks. Mr. Willey did not see the train which backed into him. That train knocked him down and severed one of his legs.

A well-known and very experienced railway claim agent lived close to the accident scene there in the town. He was called immediately by the station agent. The claim agent took pictures, before the injured conductor was even removed to the hospital. At trial, railway counsel introduced these pictures as evidence. On cross-examination, I asked the claim agent why he didn't have a picture of the cloud of steam. His answer was that he forgot to remove the lens cover for the particular picture. In my final argument to the jury, I placed a blank, white sheet of paper on the bulletin board before the jury to represent the missing picture of the cloud of steam. The jury got the message. We received a very large verdict for the four days of conscious pain and suffering Mr. Willey had endured before he died. Chief Surgeon Dr. Emmett, of the C&O Hospital in Clifton Forge, Virginia, gave strong personal testimony on this point.

His widow, Nell Willey, had come to the courthouse in downtown Roanoke for the several-day trial, driving her Cadillac automobile and parking in front of the courthouse. Railway chief counsel was George Cochran, a hoity-toity lawyer from an "old family" in Staunton, Virginia. He was later a Virginia Supreme Court Justice. In his final argument to the jury he made a reference to Mrs. Willey's Cadillac. When the jury returned its decision, we received such a large verdict that the trial judge, Ted Dalton, said it was "shocking" and "should be reduced."

"Miss" Nell Willey was a most respected and impressive witness and client. After the trial, in the hallway outside the courtroom, a woman approached Mrs. Willey. She had been one of our jurors. She touched Mrs. Willey's arm, leaned towards her and said, "Honey, I have a Cadillac, too."

Members of the Willey family have remained my lifetime friends. This kind of reward you just don't get defending large companies or the insurance industry.

James Morris Versus
the C&O Railway Company

Yet another Summers County spinoff case was one for a railway worker on the C&O Railroad Yard at Raceland, Kentucky. Here everything was done at double-time. He was particularly accident prone. He had a reputation of having sustained more injuries than all of the other workers around him. I brought suit in Charleston. The railroad only offered us five thousand dollars. At the end of the first day, they came up to eight thousand dollars. We declined this offer and proceeded to try our complete case.

My client had a very attractive young wife and three young, well-behaved children in courtroom; the family having no other place to go nor any babysitters on hand. The young counsel for the railroad was taking his orders from the headquarters legal office of the railroad in Baltimore and he was directed to prove all of the prior accidents of this plaintiff to show he was a stumblebum of some kind. I brought in a lawyer who had earlier been an associate of mine, George Daugherty. George now lived in the Charleston area. We decided to let the railroad go ahead and prove these prior accidents although they weren't exactly relevant to this particular case. After they proved these other accidents, we simply asked our client had he ever filed a claim for injury or damages against the railroad for any of them. He said he had never done so and the record confirmed that fact. We won a very handsome verdict. He died recently. Our office worked to settle his very respectable estate for the benefit of the children who had sat through the trial when the railway persecuted their father those many years before.

Railway Spinoffs

As a result of these railroad cases, and the fact that I had been Damon Williams lawyer, I got a reputation as a "go-to-court" trial lawyer. A rash of railway employee cases came to me as a major part of my practice for a few years.

These railroad employees were friends of Damon Williams. Because of Damon's friendship, sincerity and popularity, they had faith in me as a lawyer to keep their interests uppermost; to keep them informed; and, to work closely with them with complete loyalty, partiality and devotion to their interests; like an old-fashioned doctor did and still should do.

The U.S. Supreme Court had established that certain railway employee lawyers had the right to solicit cases that fell under the "Federal Employers Liability Act." This act established the rule of "Comparative Negligence" in cases of employees injured on the job as railroaders. The Supreme Court decision declared that the Federal Act was not understood nor adequately prosecuted by the run-of-the-mill lawyers. The court implied that only "specialists" in this field were competent.

The passage of this Federal Law was politically designed to halt wholesale tyranny of the railroads in the treatment of their injured employees' claims. The practical result was that a few lawyers in certain big cities polished their images up to a high degree and teamed up with the railway "Brotherhood"/Union. Practically all of the cases became channeled, wholesale, to a few big-name, big-city lawyers. Just like my Hatcher case for my old boyhood friend, these "bigshot" lawyers "wheeled and dealed" with these cases. They had no real personal regard for, or knowledge of, the individual client.

The railway claim agent, like a wolf in sheep's clothing, tried to develop an instant buddy relationship with any railway employee who became injured or crippled. He would appear and become their new "best friend." The Virginian Railway claims agent's first name was hardly known to the railway men, but his nickname, "Slick," was known to all. He was the railway company's person assigned to "help" the injured employee. However, his bread was buttered, one hundred percent, by the railway.

In the numerous cases I tried in the courts of two states against the Virginian, the N&W and C&O Railroads, I scored unusually high verdicts. As a result of making this record of trial recoveries, the most personable claim agents of both nearby railways became extremely friendly. They tested me out in the settlement of a number of cases prior to bringing suit. Despite this onslaught of intense friendliness, my demands remained high and my goal that the recovery should fit the injury unshaken.

At the same time, I was given advice by some of my clients and trial witnesses, who were fellow railroaders and well connected in the "Brotherhood" or friends of the local union officers. I was told that I should visit the central or regional "Brotherhood" officers and work out some kind of relationship with them. By that method that I might be recommended by them to the membership for these cases. Thus, was the road traveled by the "bigshot" lawyers disclosed to me; these "bigshots" who had already cornered the market.

I would not follow this path, which I felt compromised my clients' interests and made me, in effect, a double-agent. I would not settle the claims at bargain prices and compromise my partisanship.

And so, my season in this lucrative practice played out. One of the most able and personable trainee lawyers in my firm split with me, and I with him. I let him go because I felt he wanted to take my place at the head of the firm prematurely. In light of the Supreme Court decision, I did not challenge this false system of case generation. My ex-employee set his own shop up and started advertising all over the air waves that railway cases were his specialty. I can only speculate what arrangements he may have cultivated with the claim agents and the "Brotherhood" chiefs.

Following this pattern of the railway cases, the process of channeling cases is going on more and more in all types of tort litigation across the land. At present, certain lawyers build their images on a national scale through television media as experts and consultants in certain fields of law. The infamous O.J. Simpson circus served as a prolific breeding ground for such "super-lawyers."

At this writing, a team of such "specialists" are being challenged by the West Virginia State Bar with reference to their practice of soliciting all manner of major tort cases in West Virignia. They contact our citizents by long-distance telephone calls from their Washington, DC offices. This is "ambulance chasing" on a national scale. These fakers resemble the television evangelists that are trying to take all church contributions away from local churches. It remains to be seen how far this erosion will go to destroy the virtue of the practice of law.

PRACTICE
PROLIFERATES

Firing Incompetent Counsel
in Virginia

A case which I am very proud of, was sent to me by the West Virginia State president of the NAACP. I had a great respect for the dynamic president of this organization. He was a very well known Huntington lawyer and a member of the West Virginia Trial Lawyers Association. I was flattered that he would send his cousin to me as a client.

His cousin wanted to see what I could do to rescue his case from a lawyer he had previously employed in Luray, Page County, Virginia. The client lived in Fayette County, about half way between my southern-most county seat and the state capital in Charleston, W.V. He was U.S. mail carrier in his hometown of Fayetteville. In addition he was well known over a several state area as a talented musician with his own musical group. He had several times played with large circuses and often played at major city clubs and in concerts. He was a very accomplished pianist. I was also impressed with his attractive and self-possessed wife, who was the daughter of a Methodist clergyman from the eastern shore of Maryland. These young people were both elegant and college educated. And, despite their accomplishments, they were quite modest.

They were represented in Luray by a middle-aged "A-rated" attorney, who was a graduate of my University of Virginia Law School. I called him and wrote him a series of letters to get him to move the matter along. I detected a certain arrogance and air of importance about this lawyer. He had a subtle reluctance to prosecute the case of an out-of-state black man in the Page County Court. The stuffy fellow seemed a classic estate lawyer, and not at all a trial lawyer. Therefore, I proceeded to personally visit Luray, sizing up the situation and conferring with a potential replacement local attorney.

I found a contemporary fellow marine lawyer named Robey Janney, who had been raised in Giles County, across the state line in Virginia from my West Virginia County of Mercer, West Virginia. Robey's young son was practicing with him and was making quite a name for himself in the local courts. I watched this young lawyer in the courtroom in Page County and, thereafter, decided to associate young Janney. I discharged the hoity-toity old lawyer who looked down his nose at my client.

We proceeded to get a very nice award by suing the tour bus company who crossed our client's automobile path while he was passing through the Luray Cavern vacation area and, thereby, clobbered our client's car and roughed him up considerably in the process.

I got a particular amount of pleasure in this engagement and found out that my young associate, and the great majority of Virginians serving as jurors in Page County, were very ready to do justice by my black client. He appeared in court, our intelligent client, accompanied by his modest and good-looking wife, represented by a persistent, determined and well-mannered team of lawyers from Virginia and West Virginia.

Divorces

After World War II, divorces, previously rather rare, became rampant in the land. Most lawyers had many divorce clients. I have tried innumerable divorce cases in my county and surrounding counties. I don't remember most of these cases, however, I do remember the cases in which I patched up the marriage and, instead of gaining a fee, gained loyal, lifetime clients and friends.

In those cases I was more counselor than hired gun. The parties felt free to call me at all hours of the day or night. Sometimes I would get both parties into the office and referee as they aired their differences. In a departure from my normal role as adversary, I would stay neutral in the affray, pointing out strengths and faults on each side. I can think of at least three couples who used me as a mediator for years, staying together through thick and thin. They and their children remain my loyal friends.

Many cases involved drinking problems, however, financial difficulties and unemployment were frequently factors. One of the best jobs in the southern counties was railroad employment.

Several women clients lost their railroad employee husbands, for a period of time, when some greedy widow or unmarried woman wooed them away. I advised these women to tough it out, to thwart the rival and not give up the husband. Absent the woman giving in, the husband would have no grounds. Old Judge Nickel Kramer strictly required grounds before granting a divorce. I recall several of these women clients who waited out their wayward husbands. After a time, their husbands came back home very humbled and the marriages resumed.

One of my favorite couples were old family friends, a car dealer in town, and his wife, who was also the dealership book-keeper. I helped keep them together. I have remained friends with both of them ever since.

Jury Research and Local Prejudice

This same woman, the wife of the car dealer in Princeton, was injured in an accident. She was rear-ended by a wholesale delivery truck. The truck was owned by Carolina Markets, head-quartered in neighboring Raleigh County. We brought suit in Raleigh when we were unable to get service of process in Mercer County where the accident occurred.

This was a case of clear liability and real damages. The question was not if we would win the case, but by how much. I was stunned when that Raleigh County jury returned a verdict for the defendant.

I later discovered that a hidden factor had played a role with the jury. A factor I could have explored during jury selection had I known. I had failed to study the background of the wholesale grocery owner, the defendant. It turned out he was one of U.S. Senator, Robert C. Byrd's best supporters and faithful contributors. Senator Byrd had worked as a meat cutter in one of this fellow's stores before he skyrocketed to fame in politics. Senator Byrd is revered in Raleigh County. The defendant's connection with him was well known. However, I had failed to discover it. As a result, I lost a case I should have won. All because of a hidden factor.

A similar disaster befell me and my West Virginia client when we sued for injuries from a truck collision in Wytheville, Virginia. The defense was represented by the local firm of Campbell & Campbell. Old Stuart Campbell, Sr., was head of the local bank. His office was upstairs, over the bank, with an entrance off the vestibule of the bank's lobby. He didn't even have a sign on the street level or building front. Everyone knew where he held forth, and, every farmer in that cattle farm country de-pended on his bank in the off seasons. Trying that case was downright eerie, where we sensed all through the trial that the jury was simply not buying our foreigner's case.

Virginians tend to look down their noses at West Virginians. Nowhere is this more pronounced than in Virginia counties bordering West Virginia. In fact, cases of West Virginians against Virginians in the immediately adjoining Virginia counties were pretty well doomed because of this prejudice. If our West Virginia client sued further inland in Virginia in more metropolitan areas and, especially in Federal Courthouses, we had better reception.

One case in Roanoke, my West Virginia client named Annie Laurie Davis, had a back injury. Our case was in Federal Court against the Falwell Fast Freight Trucking Company of Lynchburg, Virginia, whose truck rear ended my client at a stoplight in the middle of the county seat town of Pearisburg neighboring Giles County, Virginia. The case was defended by Lynwood Holton, who later became governor of Virginia. I took some very effective photos of the stoplight at the scene from the second story of a building on the corner intersection, where the pictures looked down on the intersection and was very effective in proving the Fast Freight heedlessness. After the recovery of a nice verdict, my client, Annie Laurie, left her mountaineer husband and moved to Florida. A nice old lady on the jury came up to me in the courtroom after the verdict was announced and told me I reminded her of her son who had died a few years earlier. This time a hidden factor had worked for me.

The Demonstration
that Backfired

Another case stands as an exception to the state border prejudice situation. It also stands out as an example of what not to do with demonstrative evidence.

My client was William Lee, a very fine and respected black citizen from McComas, in the coalfield area of Mercer County. He sued the black Elks Lodge of Pocahontas, across the state line in Virginia. Mr. Lee was very dignified at the trial, which was held in the Tazewell County Courthouse. I associated "Big John" Gillespie of Tazewell as co-counsel.

Crockett Hughes represented the Elks Lodge. Crockett made

the fatal mistake of putting on a demonstration in the court-room without trying it out beforehand in a barn or some other out-of-the-way place.

The case was about an injury Mr. Lee sustained when being initiated as a new member in the Elks Lodge. Part of the ceremony involved being struck with a paddle. The initiation went awry during the paddling and my client was injured as a result.

Defense counsel called the grand archon or dragon or high potentate leader of the lodge as his star witness. This witness intended to show that the whole affair was innocent and harmless. The giant fellow held the ceremonial paddle in one hand. As in the initiation, there was a blank .30 calibre cartridge inserted into the paddle. He dramatically whammed the charged paddle into the large palm of his other hand. He was careful to turn the face of it outward, away from him, where the force of the discharge went into the atmosphere.

Acoustics in the upstairs courtroom could not have been more to my liking. The explosion of the blank shell upon impact resonated through the courtoom, throughout the courthouse and into the street. This caused a great commotion. The high sheriff came running up the stairway to the courtroom. People came off the streets to the courtroom. Even old Supreme Court Justice Buchannan, who had his office in the courthouse when not on duty in Richmond, came in. Everybody ran into the courtroom. The judge finally restored order in the court, but the fate of the grand and benevolent Elks Lodge was sealed.

One of the jurors asked the judge if the jury, consisting entirely of white males, might see the injury. The injury had only been described by doctor's reports during the trial. We gladly assented to that request. Mr. Lee, both counsel, the judge and the jury all repaired to the privacy of the jury room. There, Mr. William Lee let down his pants. The jury observed a very bad scar which the initiation explosion had imposed upon his gluteus maximus. We received a handsome verdict accordingly. The wrong was thus righted and the Grand Benevolent Order of the Elks Lodge was brought low into the valley of humility.

Doing the Best Thing
for a Young Client

A case I probably spent more time on than any other, had no big payday at the end but gave me more moral satisfaction than the cases in which I obtained large verdicts and got large fees. Because of the confidential nature of the matter, I will not name my young client. When he was a mere babe, his mother divorced her alcoholic army husband. She came to my office and showed me the most gruesome pictures of her young male child taken following surgical procedures performed by a local urologist to correct the birth defect of a deformed penis. The doctor was reportedly drunk or seriously hung over during the surgery. The results shown in the colored photographs spoke volumes about his butchery of this young child.

His mother hired me to bring an action against the surgeon for the malpractice and permanent deformity of the young boy. The major claim, for lifetime permanent damage, belonged to the boy himself. He could have asserted such claim as a child by the appointment of a guardian ad litem, or he could wait until he was of legal age and bring suit. In the meantime, it was the mother's duty to help him achieve maximum recovery and the best possible correction of the butchered organ. The costs of such corrective procedures and the boy's physical pain in the process would have justified a huge recovery from eventual trial of the case.

I was able, with the aid of different charitable institutions, to find the most skillful surgery specialists in the land and to find sources to pay for the long series of corrective surgery. This effort spanned a period of years while the boy was growing up.

My only compensation was a contingent percentage of the claim when the end result and maximum cure was able to be effected. During these years, while the boy was growing up, his widowed grandfather taught him how to fish in my farm pond and elsewhere. Then the grandfather married a younger woman. This took him away from his family and the boy. The young man had gotten an attachment to me and my ample fish pond and continued to fish there and to bring other boys there to fish. He was approaching legal age. The excellent treating surgeons were making very good progress on plastic surgery restoration and reconstruction in this vital growth period of time.

In school he was very bashful about going to the public toilet, since his male organ was not yet functioning normally. He had great psychological difficulty adjusting on the playground and, finally, in dating girls. I was able to give him encouragement along the way. He was willing to discuss his problems with me, problems he couldn't discuss with his own mother. I had raised two sons and two daughters, all somewhat older than this young man.

Slowly, the young man gained personal physical confidence. He was becoming a very handsome young man. The girls who began to come along kept their interest in him. Finally, he came to realize he was normal and able. After one or two failed attempts, he found the right girl. She had married the wrong person first and had two children before marrying my young friend.

The young man and his wife have three handsome children and they have moved to North Carolina, where he is happily employed. His mother recently died of her persistent Myasthenia Gravis disease, having kept in touch with me over the years as her son was achieving maximum recover.

The crisis in the legal case was in electing between pursuing damages in court, including psychological damages, or choosing not to put the boy through such an ordeal. It would have been a major trial and would have centered on his psychological impairment. Psychiatrists were available to testify to the permanent mental damage. The boy could have lapsed into becoming a basket case of self-pity if money was our object. I could have gone to court for a major money recovery, but with a totally destroyed individual on the threshold of his adult life. The choice was easy for me and I received a rare personal reward to see this fine young man choose the positive course and put the idea of a lawsuit out of his mind and out of his life.

I amassed a tremendous file dealing with the doctors and the young man and his mother. My satisfaciton was in helping this young man grow up to become a model citizen and family man, the pride of his devoted mother. My son Henry, who is now practicing in our office, is helping the young man settle the affairs of his mother's modest estate.

Lawyers are not always skunks, sometimes they are missionaries.

The Junk Yard Versus the Blue Chip Corporation

In my retirement years, I often take a hike about 6:30 a.m. through a large public graveyard close to my home. In my walk, I pass by the graves of Silas Floyd Fuller and other members of his family, including S.F. Fuller, Jr., all often adorned with fresh flowers.

Silas Fuller came to Princeton many years ago from southwestern Virginia. He started a junk yard in "Stumpy Bottom," on the outskirts of Princeton near the rail yard. This is where all of the horse traders lived and trained and traded their horses.

He gradually built a junkyard out of boards and tar paper, adding shacks and storage areas gradually until it spread over a couple of acres of ground. He traded in every kind of scrap imaginable, including hides and grease from restaurant kitchens and ginseng from all of the wooded hillsides 'roundabout. A chain link fence and a junkyard dog provided security for the sprawling enterprise.

The only one of these interconnected shacks that was heated was Fuller's personal office. It was heated by stove fired by propane gas. A propane storage tank stood beside the outside wall of the one-room office. A salesman replenished the gas at regular intervals. Each time he did so, he disconnected and reconnected the copper line connecting the tank to the stove. Late one winter night, the entire junkyard went up in flames. By morning Fuller's Junkyard had been reduced to ashes.

It wasn't too long before Mr. Fuller came to my office. He hired me to represent him and bring suit over the destruction of his business. I expect that Mr. Fuller had consulted other and older lawyers in the area and had been turned down. He might have heard of me from one of the many elderly men I taught in the Sunday School of the largest church in the town. He may have heard that I was a sucker for a hard luck case. I liked the old man and saw him as a man of great virtue and industry.

We would sue the Union Carbide Corporation (owned by the DuPont corporation), who had provided the propane tank and serviced the stove hook-up. We accused their salesman of responsibility in causing the disastrous fire. We sued to recover the value of all that had been lost. However, there was a total absence of tangible evidence on the value of the loss. All of his records and inventories were completely burned in his office. The only record of the contents, and the value of the same, was in his brain.

Because of the complete destruction, the issue of causation was contested by Union Carbide. We would go to trial with both issues, causation and damages, completely in doubt.

We brought suit in Federal District Court in Abingdon, Virginia. District Court was held in courthouses around the several cities of western Virginia. The minimum jurisdiction of Federal Court was ten thousand dollars. We requested damages in the precise sum of fifteen thousand dollars plus some odd dollars and cents.

Union Carbide had refused to consider any settlement of the claim. They made no offers whatsoever. This "blue-chip" corporation was represented by a Bluefield attorney, two New York based lawyers and by the firm of Penn and Stuart of Abingdon, Virginia. The defense counsel table seemed rather crowded with lawyers determined to prevail aginst my client, the solitary "Old Man" Fuller.

We went to trial for three days in the Federal Courthouse at Abingdon. Judge Barksdale, of Lynchburg, was the presiding judge. I associated the Federal District Attorney, old family friend Howard Gilmer, Jr., of Pulaski, Virginia, as our local counsel.

We elected to try the plaintiff's case without a jury and the defense agreed. During the trial the senior member of the Penn and Stuart law firm, a direct descendant of famous Confederate General Jeb Stuart, would appear in the courtroom. Had we tried the case before a local jury, many of the jurors would have been impressed with this man, and impressed by the presence of the big city lawyers allied with the local lawyers and politicians. The judge, however, was known by my co-counsel to be a very independent person from old line Lynchburg, and not so easily impressed by the lawyers on the hustings and their New York allies.

Each evening, counsel for both sides retired to their rooms at the historic Martha Washington Inn, in Abingdon. Howard would spend a lot of time with the defense lawyers, having after-dinner cocktails and such. Meanwhile I would retire to my room and work diligently to prepare for the next day of trial.

Our theory of liability was that the fire was caused when

the propane salesman created a leak in the propane line. The agent was the only one who ever serviced the heating system. There was a sign placed on the system warning others not to tamper with it. Over a period of time he had regularly bent the copper pipe from the tank to the stove, each time at the same place. Gradually a small leak had developed, not far from the stove.

The copper line was one of the few things to survive the fire. Ironically, it had remained immune to the fire by virtue of the nature of the cold liquid propane gas within the line. The portion of the line from the tank to the break was our "Exhibit A" proof of the cause of the fire.

The "best evidence" of the value of the damages lay solely in the brain of my client. "Old Man" Fuller made a most wonderful and impressive witness by enumerating the items in great detail. He recited the cost and value of even the smallest items in a thorough inventory. He had prepared the list strictly from memory. The aggregate value was the exact amount for which we had brought suit.

The judge found in favor on liability and then rendered a verdict on damages in the precise amount testified to by the old man.

Judge Barksdale had been an infantry commander in France in World War I. He had seen some of the fiercest fighting in that war. The old commander had not been overly impressed with the self-important array of defense lawyers, who were so confident our junkyard case had no merit.

My one-third contingency fee was shared with my local counsel. With his ten thousand dollars, plus his recoverable costs, "Old Man" Fuller rebuilt his junkyard and quickly scrounged up a new junk collection for resale. Better than that, he got a new lease on life by beating the giant "blue-chip" corporation. Now he was holding his head high in the community.

His son, S.F. Fuller, Jr., later built another larger junkyard. The father/son team was very successful and diligent in their business.

The son and daughter-in-law later established a very profitable "R.V." park, just off the new Interstate, with every first class modern amenity. His son became a respected deacon in the large First Baptist Church, but, tragically, died fairly young of a heart attack. His wife still runs the park. It is she who regularly places flowers on the graves of her husband and his father, my most credible client, S.F. Fuller.

Coming from the remote countryside of southwestern Virginia, and starting from nothing, Silas Fuller had risen to establish himself, and his family, as a most reliable and respected member of this community.

Product Liability Summary

Liability cases involving defective products that produce harm to innocent users are few and far between. However, when such cases are prosecuted they often produce the good result of increasing product safety – the good old American free enterprise way.

Product liability in the courtroom is purely a battle of experts – the freewheeling professors from universities across the land versus corporate engineers. Hired by the giant manufacturers to concoct their various and sundry products and gadgets, these engineers come to court to defend why the product didn't work the way it was supposed to, or why some hazard wasn't foreseen.

I had a case many years ago for a young man who stepped on the cover of a water meter and broke his leg. I settled the case before trial at a fair figure and didn't hazard a jury trial. My client was young and his leg had healed well. His lack of a real good occupation cut his loss claim down. Also, there's some question why he was out there stepping on water meter covers in the first place.

All water meter covers over the entire land of America were made at that time with their lids sitting loosely on the top of a rounded enclosure. I am confident this booby trap design was the basis for other, more serious cases across the land.

Thanks to the law of product liability, I have noticed all over the country the advances in design and engineering of water meter tops – they are screwed down – and many, many other consumer products have followed the same course.

Product liability cases are expensive to litigate. The corporate giant will go to the greatest expense, paying experts an hourly fee and hiring giant law firms. All this rather than to admit that they goofed in designing or making the product. They will spend countless dollars to persuade the national and state legislatures to restrict lawsuits. Wishing to escape liability for their manufacturing ineptitude they claim that making them liable makes products too expensive.

Homeowners' Liability

When I started my practice the insurance industry was small. Coverage for automobiles and other types of liability was minimal. Over the years the industry has grown and prospered. Coverage has broadened to insure against possible harm in new areas of risk. The change has been dramatic since I began my practice of the law of torts.

The industry had expanded from coverage of fire, windstorm etc., to include all possible negligent harm on the premises of their insured. This expansion reflects a public policy which favors full compensation for those who suffer harm whatever the setting. The best example of such expanded insurance coverage is the prevalence of homeowners' insurance. These policies are often written so broadly as to insure against harm in many settings.

My first case where the claim was made under a homeowners' policy illustrates the problems created when an injured party begins dealing with an insurance company before contacting a lawyer.

I represented a pretty young married woman who suffered a ruptured disc in her lower back. While on a camping trip, she and her young executive husband were guests of their best friends at that couple's riverside cabin. The two couples were sitting in canvas folding chairs cooking-out on the riverbank in front of the cabin. The father of the host, a jaunty old man, dropped in on the group. He playfully came up behind my beautiful young client where she was sitting and folded her up in the chair, lifting her and the chair completely off the ground. The young lady tried not to act offended. Being the polite and considerate guest of her best friends, she played down her injury.

However, days later her back continued to give her pain. Finally, she went to a hospital in Bluefield and consulted a neurosurgeon. Unfortunately, this neurosurgeon, just as his neurosurgeon father before him, had his bread buttered primarily by the insurance industry. The surgeon actually operated on the young lady to remove or repair a ruptured lumbar (low back) disc – the cushion between the vertebrae.

At the trial, he testified he was doubtful that the disc was completely ruptured. He claimed that the young lady wanted the surgery and that he had performed the surgery upon her insistence. I lost the case partially because of the weak medical testimony, which cast some doubt on my client's sincerity. A bigger problem had been created by the insurance adjuster, who had handled the claim, and compounded by a very skillful defense lawyer. Unfortunately they had a wide-open field to investigate and negotiate the claim, prior to my being employed.

As a result, my preparation for trial was severely hampered. My opportunity to "woodshed" the client and witnesses, a practice which is the duty of a competent lawyer, was almost completely preempted. Before my client had sought legal help, the adjuster had caused his insured, the friends and former hosts, to believe that my client and her husband were out to ruin them financially. They were told my client wanted money over and above their liability insurance coverage.

The long-standing friendship of these young couples was ruined. The jury got the impression from defense testimony that the defendants were going to lose their home and everything they owned in defending against the claim.

A Matter of Tactics

In my other cases involving homeowner insurance coverage, I have been able to head off such defense tactics. I immediately inform my client, to assure their friends, the defendant homeowners, who are often relatives or close friends, that they have no desire to claim recovery beyond their insurance coverage. These policies are written to cover both friends and strangers. They are meant to benefit guests in the home. In fact, total strangers, called trespassers or non-invitees, are excluded from coverage by the law and the terms of the policy.

Having been burned by this deception I learned a valuable lesson. I learned to head off these tactics of creating hard feelings and playing people off against each other. I recall two cases of grandchild against grandfather, where, working against the same insurance team I prevented attempts to foster hard feelings in these families.

An old farmer in Summers County was being visited by his

very attractive married daughter and several of her children at his farm on the Greenbrier River. Her infant son of about six, his cousins and some neighbors living nearby, were playing "Follow the Leader" through the farm buildings. They climbed in the window of a small shed that was otherwise locked. Inside there were several very old dynamite blasting caps, which the grandfather farmer had failed to dispose of after he had dynamited stumps to clear his fields years before.

An anvil and a hammer were nearby. The boy put a copper blasting cap on the anvil and hit it with the hammer. His hand and eye were injured by fragments from the explosion. When the mother consulted me, I told her to leak it back in the family to the homeowner grandfather that the insurance coverage sold to him by the defense was to cover family, as well as strangers, and that she did not want recovery beyond such coverage. We won the case and the family stayed on good terms. I have been a friend of this wonderful family ever since. The boy has grown up nicely – a fine looking young man, although still scarred by a defective hand and an injured eye.

Monroe County Courthouse at Union.

214

The Hines Case

Another similar case involved old Mr. Hines, also a grandfather. He owned a farm located on a road named for his highly-respected old family in the beautiful countryside of neighboring Monroe County.

One day old farmer Hines had charge of his beautiful four-year-old grandson. They were in the area of the barn, on the grandfather's nice homestead. Mr. Hines had given the boy a ride in his lap on a large new farm tractor. Momentarily, the grandfather got off the tractor to get a tool out of the shed. He deposited the boy on the ground and left the tractor motor running. In this moment of inattention, the very bright, alert and inquisitive boy observed the generator of the tractor revolving and put his finger into the opening, where the moving gears were visible. The resulting injury caused an ugly and permanently disfiguring wound to the little boy's finger.

The father of the child consulted me. The first thing I told him was that he should advise the grandfather that his home insurance policy was meant to benefit family or neighbors who were injured on the premises.

The rule of law is that the insured is required to cooperate with his insurance company. An insured is not to admit liability or collude with claimants on liability. In other words all parties are to be strictly on their best behavior. A good, proper settlement for this claim was effected. Peace and good feelings were maintained within the family and they have remained my strong friends since.

The mother of the child, a good-looking woman and a most intelligent and respected school teacher, later became my client when she received a facial injury in an automobile collision. A car in front of her vehicle had turned to enter a filling station when another car came head-on into her lane, at a high rate of speed. The crash caused a deviated septum of the nose to her beautiful face. We recovered the largest verdict that any woman had ever received in the Circuit Court of Monroe County up to that time. This lovely school teacher and mother was an ace client, keeping her box of Kleenex tissue handy at the trial. Her medical evidence was most sympathetic on the permanent effects of her injury. Seven of the twelve jurors were women who identified with my popular client. The unhappy defendant was

215

a young lawyer flying low and late to a political event when the accident happened. The other defendant and pickup truck who drove across the lane of the flying lawyer and stopped at a service station without being physically involved in the collision. From the outset, in opening statements, I asked the jury to give a full and adequate verdict, regardless of whether they felt one or both of the other drivers were at fault. They put it all on the low-flying lawyer. Both drivers were insured by the same insurance company (my old friend) – Nationwide – but, of course, had separate attorneys defending each driver.

One Case Leads to Another: More Facial Injuries

Kay Hines' outstanding verdict in conservative Monroe County led to another face injury case involving the wife of one of the defendants in Kay's case.

This client was the wife of the driver of the pick-up truck that had turned into the filling station right before Kay was struck and so seriously injured. She was also the niece of George Shumate, owner of a local furniture store and a stalwart member of my Sunday school class.

This wife, Yvonne Dunn, hired me to bring suit for injuries she sustained in Giles County, Virginia. She had been on her way home to Monroe County from her job as secretary to the manager of the Celanese Chemical plant near Pearisburg, Virginia. Her car had been crowded off the road and into a light pole.

Mrs. Dunn received a severe facial injury caused by the impact when she struck the dashboard of her car. Her face had served as a shock absorber, protecting her brain in this accident, but leaving a profound injury. She was subjected to extensive facial surgery in Giles County hospitals.

In proving the extent, and the premanence of her injury, I sent her to New York to be examined by the doctor who wrote the accepted seven volume textbook on maxilo-facial surgeries. In this type of surgery dental surgeons and neurosurgeons combine their skills to reconstruct the maze of bones and tissue that make up the face. Yvonne was a heroic patient and an ideal client. We received a very outstanding recovery. Yvonne's numerous far-flung Shumate family, of our New River territory, remain always our best of clients.

It was a regular practice of our office, as in the Damon Williams case, to get an independent medical evaluation of our plaintiff's injuries from a non-treating physician or surgeon. This often would prove the permanent results of the injury to be worse, and often much worse, than the treating doctor of surgeon thought. Treating doctors always think they had effected the magic cure. The treating doctors didn't always think our practice in this respect was kosher. However, we knew our duty was to the client and the treating doctors had to respect us for doing our job.

The Tragic Case
of a College Student

Another outstanding case involving facial injury was that of a local college student. The case was sent to me by Jim Blume, the high sheriff of Summers County and a close friend of Damon Williams.

The young student of Concord College, in Athens, West Virginia was from Possum Hollow near Hinton in Summers County. He was the first of his family to go to college. His father was a highly-respected C&O, (now CSX) railroad engineer and his mother, fine person and a member of one of the oldest families.The boy was a hero to his younger sister and the pride of the family, which included a widowed grandmother living nearby.

The accident occurred at an intersection on the U.S. 460 divided bypass, near Bluefield. A truck coming from the interstate failed to stop for a red light. The student, who had the right-of-way, could not avoid striking the truck. He sustained a most extensive face injury in the resulting crash. The surgery required to rearrange and repair the structures of his face generated astronomical medical bills.

The facial reconstruction changed his appearance permanently. A team of skilled doctors had done their best. Despite the best care medical science could provide, the result was a different face than the young college student had before. This caused the young man great emotional disturbance, which compounded problems he already had.

He recovered a large sum of money as a result of this lawsuit. We counseled and persuaded him to bank the money. He agreed to save and then properly invest the money.

Our fee in this case was spent in building an addition to our office. The large conference room on the top floor and enlarged office area beneath are due to this case. A brass plaque at the entrance to the spacious conference room dedicates the annex to this young man. That room serves for depositions but is especially useful for initial conferences with prospective clients. Here as many of our trial lawyers as are available sit in to evaluate cases at the first interview with a prospective client.

The student had been having identity problems before the accident. He was a sensitive young man. He felt outclassed by boys from more affluent backgrounds in the social fraternities. At least this thought was in his mind. We all hoped the large recovery would help him to build a more positive self image.

Not long after receiving his award, he met, and married, a pretty young girl who helped him quickly waste his money. He divorced the girl and married the right girl and has two fine children, but needs further corrective surgery, with his award exhausted.

Long-Term Client Relations

The greatest compliment of my law career came from the Reverend Billy Apostolon, of Hinton. A few years after my Damon Williams victory, Billy told me, "Two people I really believe in are Jesus Christ and William Sanders." At that time, he was sweetening me up either to take his wife's "whiplash" case, or to get me involved in some of his local Summers County crusades.

He was a most energetic preacher and was also a school teacher. It was hard to tell which career was his primary means of livelihood. His father had been an immigrant Greek restauranteur in the heyday of the C&O Railroad. Then Hinton was a boom town. His father married a native Summers County girl and bought a nice farm in the lovely countryside. Here, two sons, Billy and Demitrius were raised.

With friends like this, my plaintiff's practice grew.

Billy's wife's sister was married to a Lilly, of that most numerous southern West Virginia family. The sister lived in the neighboring county of Raleigh, on Maple Fork Road. Her son, Curtis Lilly, Jr., married a young lady named Barley, whose father was the well-known and very popular gospel preacher, who regularly preached on the radio and was a founder of the Appalachian Bible College in Raleigh County, near Beckley. He was also the president of the county commission at one time.

Curtis Junior, was injured when a car crowded him off the Maple Fork Road. I tried his personal injury case in the Raleigh County Circuit Court in Beckley. Some of the family members sat as spectators in the courtroom. They sat to my rear, where I didn't notice them. They were, however, in plain view of the jury and apparently sat there eating peanuts and popcorn. The judge, for some reason, overlooked their conduct and didn't reprimand them. Aside from this group, the courtroom was fairly empty of spectators. The jury, accordingly, rendered a verdict for the defense instead of for my apparently frivolous clientele.

I appealed on the grounds that the verdict was plainly contrary to the evidence. The West Virginia Supreme Court agreed and ordered a new trial. At the second trial in the Circuit Court I did a better job of woodshedding my witnesses, and their family spectators, on their conduct in the courtroom and courthouse generally. This time around we won the case. I enjoy favorable relations with this popular Raleigh County family of Barleys and Lillys and their many kindred and friends.

All of these many country clients and clientele were generated through the widespread influence of my lifetime star client, Damon Williams, the dynamic Ford salesman. Damon's brother was a popular policeman in the city of Beckley. One of his good friends was the Honorable Harold Hank, a former state trooper who became the chief clerk of the Circuit Court in Raleigh County. I am confident that a number of my best cases in Raleigh County had received his endorsement. When he retired as chief clerk, he served as magistrate in the small court trials, trying more cases than the other several magistrates combined. When he played out, as a result of an injury, he employed my office in his social security disability claim. He was a fine man, who worked too hard and just burned himself out in his public service. His wife was secretary for the State Farm Insurance

Company in the Beckley office.

The Psychological Factor

In my early days of my practice I defended State Farm Automobile Insurance Company on several back and neck injury cases. I employed, as my expert witness, Doctor Gayle Crutchfield, chief of the department of Neurosurgery at the University of Virginia. An injury of the back or neck is like a headache and hard to prove or disprove. Such injuries can't be seen like a broken leg or a flesh wound. Therefore, back and neck injuries are prone to "psychological overlay," where the hope of financial gain is more prevalent than any real physical injury.

The term *whiplash* became very popular in insurance litigation. Chiropractors got into the ballgame in a big way as insurance coverage steadily grew.

In one case a middle-age woman was suing for a large sum of money for alleged lower back injury. I paid Doctor Crutchfield to drive all the way from Charlottesville the day before the trial to examine this lady at the local hospital. Doctor Crutchfield had served as chief surgeon for the Southern Railway during the early years when it was very much the vogue to sue railways for jostling their passengers. He had developed a very jaundiced eye toward such back and neck injuries.

He tesitifed at the trial in Mercer County Circuit Court that the woman was, in effect, a malingerer. He disputed the woman's injuries because the true and classical symptoms were not present on his examination.

The "high-rolling" plaintiff's attorney cross-examined Doctor Crutchfield viciously, saying, "You mean you can examine this lady the day before trial for approximately one-half hour and dispute all of the treatment and bills that she has undergone and tell this jury she is a fake?" The veteran physician, probably with more courtroom experience than the plaintiff's lawyer, remained unruffled and turned to the jury and looked them straight in the eye and replied, "In my years of treatment of these cases, it is like looking at an apple and telling it's an apple." This was talk on the jury level and they believed the doctor and rendered a defense verdict of no recovery.

It was obvious that the woman's husband, who had been

sitting eagerly on the front row of the courtroom, was the real sponsor of her "immense psychological overlay" in this very questionable physical injury.

In my early plaintiff's practice, we took the case of a young married woman from neighboring Wyoming County. She was a very pretty red-head. I assigned the case to my young associate, George Daugherty, who had the greatest capacity for sympathy of any lawyer of my acquaintance. George got the lady a very nice recovery. Many months later, the woman's husband came back to the office to see George and angrily told him that he wished he would deprogram his wife so she would quit her chronic complaints. Apparently her "psychological overlay" had grown out of all retrievable proportion. With the lady's youth and general good health, she should have gotten well sooner. Our sympathy had created a monster.

Bad Brakes and the Runaway Truck

One of our most appealing clients in the field of automobile personal injuries was Sharon Emerson of Jamestown, New York, on Chautauqua Lake.

She and her young husband had two infant children. The husband was unemployed in hard times around Jamestown. He had accompanied his uncle, a private contractor, in his uncle's very large, personally owned, tractortrailor. They would take trips to the south hauling valuable cargo. This seemed like economic salvation to the unemployed young man. He contracted to purchase his own tractor and trailer on terms of making payments out of his fees earned in hauling.

Emerson's first trip with his own rig was to haul a load of iron rods to the southern West Virginia coalfields. His wife Sharon accompanied him. They started down the now infamous three-mile-long grade down Flat Top Mountain on the West Virginia turnpike headed to Camp Creek. The brakes on the rig overheated and failed. As the emergency became clear, Emerson told his wife to crawl up into the back cabin of the tractor. The truck, and the trailer with its heavy load, plowed through the guardrails and over the high bank. Young Emerson was killed instantly. His body was horribly mangled along the guardrails.

The young wife, Sharon, survived the crash. This disaster left her with one lower leg amputated and the other foot badly and permanently crippled. She was hospitalized and treated for a long time at the new Princeton Community Hospital. There she won the sympathy of all the hospital personnel and many of the citizens of the town.

She employed our firm to wage her claim against any negligent responsible parties for her injuries. Our case was brought in the Federal District Court against the sellers of the tractor trailer as well as her late husband's estate.

One of my old college class mates, Robert Bootey, was a third generation lawyer and at the time was a municipal judge in Jamestown, New York. I associated Bob on an agreed hourly fee, win or lose, for whatever time he might spend to assist me in setting up and taking vital discovery depositions in the Jamestown area. I went up to New York several times in personal investigation and in taking the depositions. Bob Bootey's association helped open doors to me in my search for the evidence.

We proved that a certain salvage (junk) dealer had scrounged up the trailer from various old wrecked parts. We showed that he sold this pile of junk to another company who had the haulage contracts. We then proved that this company had falsified the documents on inspection of the outfit, under interstate commerce regulations. And we proved that the brakes on the trailer carrying such a heavy load were practically non-existent. The young driver/owner was duped into buying this booby trap rig which was doomed to runaway on the Flat Top Mountain course.

A large settlement resulted from all our work and preparation. Sharon Emerson remained a faithful visitor and friend of all the secretaries in our office as she took up residence in our town for a period of years.

JUDGES

Good Judges

Raleigh County Judge Berkley Lilly, now retired, is a member of the large Lilly clan of southern West Virginia. He is greatly respected by the people of his county as a good, fair and scholarly judge. He never became afflicted with the "Godalmighty Complex."

I first heard the term "Godalmighty Complex" applied by a grand old retired lawyer of my town who was beyond being reprimanded or held in contempt for such utterance. This complex afflicts many judges, especially Federal Judges, who are appointed for life and have large sycophantic staffs to attend their every need.

In my early years I knew of a certain Federal District Judge in southern West Virginia who had written his own biography before he reached his retirement. Most of the lawyers who frequented his courtroom thought it wise to buy a copy of the book from his clerk. As I remember, the theme of this book was that he was a "self-made man."

I was trying a three-day trial before this dignified self-made man at the Federal Courthouse in Bluefield shortly after he had written his book. My opponent lawyer, a leading defense attorney, lived in Bluefield. The judge's homebase was Charleston. During the week of trial, in the evenings, the judge and his wife played bridge with my opponent and his wife at their home on "Country Club Hill" in Bluefield. The judge was so perfect "in character" that he saw nothing wrong in this practice. I certainly didn't raise the issue. This same defense attorney was a principal proponent of a system of appointing judges, like they do in our sister state of Virginia, instead of electing them by the voters like we do in West Virginia.

I had a Virginia case in Alleghany County, where I represented a wholesale grocer of West Virginia who had his ninety thousand dollars account frozen in a receivership procedure brought by the retail grocer in Covington, Virginia. The local state judge, appointed by the governor on advice of the Virignia State Senate, named the local lawyer (who happened to be the state senator who got the judge his job) to serve as trustee in the receivership. The trustee/lawyer then hired an accountant to run the bankrupt three retail store outlets while the debtor spent each winter in Florida. The trustee took a monthly fee while the accountant did all the work.

This jolly little party had been going on for three years and my West Virginia wholesaler client wanted his overdue account unfrozen and paid. I knew little about receivership. I associated an old law professor at the University of Virginia, Professor T. Munford Boyd, who wrote the textbook on the subject. At the pretrial conference with the judge and counsel for the debtor (the state senator), I introduced my co-counsel, the law professor. The judge remarked, "Professor Boyd, you will find we practice Allegany County Law out here." However, the defendant promptly unfroze and paid our account, rather than allow the stalemate to end up in Virginia Supreme Court, where that same Allegany County Law would have come under severe scrutiny.

Other Favorite Judges

One of my favorite jurists was Judge C.C. Chambers, of Logan County, over in the domain where the Hatfields and McCoys shot it out in older days. In fact, one of the best lawyers I tangled with was Logan County's blind Coleman Hatfield. He was led, by his secretary to the courtroom, where he was a most formidable opponent.

Judge Chambers was a tobacco chewing judge in the best tradition of the old judges, where they had their cuspidors behind their bench and at their desk in chambers. Every member of the jury had his own private small brass cuspidor beside his seat in the jury box in the first days of my practice. Judge Chambers called them like he saw them, without hesitation, and without retiring all counsel to his chambers in the back room.

He was seldom appealed and tried all the criminal, as well as all the civil cases in Logan County. This was in my early days, when I practiced for the defense. He cut through the criminal trial docket in the morning of the first day of court by putting many accused on probation with warning that if they came before him again it would be rough going. When these accused had a prior criminal record, he told them to get out of his county and if they were ever to come back and appear before again, the jailhouse would be sitting on top of them.

In the afternoon of the first day of his court, he set the civil docket. For eight straight years, I probably tried more automobile cases in his court than all the other local lawyers combined.

This was because of a man named Eddie Stevens. Mr. Stevens was the State Farm Insurance company agent. He sold about fifty percent of all automobile insurance policies in the area. Eddie had several secretaries in the downtown upper story office in the thriving bee-hive town of Logan. They were busy writing policies for all the people he contacted on the streets, in luncheon clubs and in various activities in the town. His office walls were covered with placards of awards for sales records.

Other Model Judges

Judge Dennis Knapp presided over both the Buck Hatcher vs. Virginian Railway case and the James Morris vs. C&O Railroad case. Both were tried in his Common Pleas Court in Charleston. He had been a school teacher in his native Putnam County before attending law school. He had been elected and re-elected circuit judge as a Republican in the Democrat stronghold of Kanawha County. Later he was appointed Federal District Judge. He had a quiet and fair manner in the courtroom. He was never self righteous or prejudiced, rather he was the soul of humility. He had a contagious fairness which affected the parties and led to many settlements before trial. He is one of the best judges of my experience. His wife suffered a prolonged illness, and he attended her needs with great dedication.

Another great jurist was Judge Ted Dalton, of the Federal District Court of Western Virginia. He had wonderful control and respect in his courtroom. He had been a long-time trial lawyer before ascending the Federal bench. He knew almost everyone, the litigants and lawyers alike. Everyone was on an equal basis with him; he didn't play favorites. He could walk down the streets of any town in western Virginia and know almost everyone on a first name basis.

Circuit Judge Nickel Kramer, of Lewisburg, presided over the four county (Greenbrier, Pocahontas, Monroe and Summers) courthouses, but never got chummy with anyone, lawyer or litigant. He never owned or drove a car. He made his courthouse rounds in the car of his able four-county court reporter, Mary Morgan Gibson, or with his divorce commissioner.

Finally, Mary Morgan (after the death of her first husband) married leading trial lawyer, John Detch, of Lewisburg. But that didn't cut any ice with the judge or with the independent Mary Morgan. That new lawyer husband got the same treatment meted out to the rest of us. Judge Kramer reserved all "editorial comment" for himself. If a smart lawyer tread on this holy ground, he was asking for trouble. None of the lawyers practicing before Judge Kramer knew which side of the bed he got up on any given morning. He was not to be taken for granted.

All the best judges were real people, because they were independent people who never acquired a "Godalmighty Complex" and who didn't go around prejudging cases before they heard all sides. Every court (judge) instructs the jury to not prejudge the evidence and to not even discuss the evidence among their fellow jurors until all the evidence is in, the arguments of counsel and court's instructions are completed. Yet, many overly-righteous judges regularly practice prejudgment in their courtrooms. The word *prejudice* simply means prejudging – forming opinions before knowing the whole case of facts.

PUBLIC CAUSES

Nuclear and Solid
Waste Storage

The neighboring county of McDowell was the heart of the Pocahontas coalfield. By the later years of my law practice, the coal reserves were being mined out by sophisticated machinery. Competition from low-sulfur western coal further reduced the need for miners. The resulting unemployment caused an exodus of the population.

The Berwind family, absentee mineral rights owners, proposed that their mined-out land serve as a storage site for spent nuclear fuel rods. This nuclear waste was building up at nuclear power plants across the country. So bad was the economic situation that McDowell County leaders, and local newspapers, saw this as a panacea. The Bluefield newspaper remained quiet and did not oppose the plan. The Norfolk-Southern Railway supported the plan. For the railroad it could mean, for the first time in its history, a cargo to haul westward on the return of the coal cars from their eastern shipment to the coast. There was no apparent opposition to the grandiose plan.

The entrenched incumbent congressman was attending conventions at plush resorts with representatives of the fast growing trash-haulers national associations. The governor was silent. In this setting, I changed my political registration to Democrat and declared myself a candidate in the primary election to oppose the congressman. My sole issue was nuclear power storage in the district. This gave me standing to challenge the congressman on the issue and to challenge the governor to take a stand. Newspapers outside the coalfields abhorred the idea. The pressure brought to bear smoked out the governor and congressman and the issue was defeated.

Failing in that scheme, these absentee landowners proposed the same site to build the world's largest solid waste landfill. Again, the stuff would be hauled in the empty westbound coal cars from the coast at Norfolk, where it would be collected from the Atlantic seaboard cities for transhipment to the desolate coalfields of McDowell County. I stayed in the game with some brave coalfield grass-roots citizens and state legislation was enacted to defeat this proposal.

Newspaper Monopoly and Public School Consolidation

At the midpoint of my law practice, at about the time of the Civil Rights tempest, "Squire" Browning, an experienced newspaper man, retired from Chicago to Princeton, West Virginia, came to my office in the top of the old bank building and we initiated an attempt to break up the longstanding single family media monopoly centered in Bluefield. "Squire" Browning was the father-in-law of my old family friend, Dr. Gordon Todd, Jr., whose father and my father had come to Princeton from the University of Virginia at the same time. My father did all the legal work for Dr. Todd's hospital and he did all of our family medical work free, throughout their joint lifetimes. We got together a group of local Princeton citizens who subscribed money to found the *Princeton Times*, which started out as a "daily" and then a biweekly and then a weekly for several years before both the Princeton and Bluefield newspapers were brought up by an international chain and the whole effort went down the drain.

In the same context, I joined the rural communities to oppose the consolidation of eight county high schools into two or three large schools, requiring the students to spend hours on buses enroute to their schools. This opposition earned me the threat of the Bluefield newspaper poison pen political writer, who called me at my home one evening and told me she, "would see to it that I never amounted to anything."

On another sideline adventure, I incorporated two separate groups of my wife and eastern Virginia relatives, friends and college mates to build two separate Holiday Inn Hotels, a total of 384 rental rooms and restaurants, swimming pools and the works, which thrived for twenty-five years, but ultimately came to financial grief when roadside hotels over the entire nation became over-built and failed. My hotel investment failures caused me to sell my law office building and practice to my partners and engage in certain other public causes, including advocacy of scenic byways in the area and the writing of area historic books and attending to my home, yard and vegetable garden and, otherwise, enjoy the fruits of Kind Providence, which has sustained me through thick and thin of all things great and small.

ADDENDA

Mother at her piano in our home in her nineties.

Katherine and William at home.

234

Aerial picture of Katherine's home and flower garden.

Plaintiff Law Office Building (and the conference room upstairs on viewer's left corner.)

235

Front of Law Building – conference addition on viewer right corner of building.

Katherine and William's Children

David Hartley Sanders, Circuit Judge in Morgan, Berkeley and Jefferson counties, West Virginia (Berkeley Springs, Martinsburg and Charles Town); Mary Hylton Sanders Fowler, partner in the law firm of Huddleston, Bolen, Beatty, Porter and Copen, with offices in Huntington and Charleston, West Virginia; Katherine Todd Sanders Koerner, following career as copy editor of trade magazines for Lotus Development, now retired to homemaking in Seattle, Washington; William Henry Sanders III, partner in the law firm of Sanders, Austin, Swope and Flanigan, Princeton, West Virginia.

236

List of Lawyers Who Got Their Start in Sanders' Law Offices

Johnny Dean – Stanford University
Ben White – Washington and Lee University
Tom Lilly – North Carolina University
Pete Barrow – Washington and Lee University
Ed Brown – University of Virginia Law School
George Daugherty – West Virginia University
Odell Huffman – West Virginia University
John Troelstrup – West Virginia University
Joe Martorella – West Virginia University
Larry Winter – West Virginia University
Roger Graham – West Virginia University
John Frazier – West Virginia University
Mason Sproul – University of Virginia
Dale Sanders – Summer Intern – George Mason University
*Lane Austin – University of Kentucky Law School
Mike Gibson – University of Richmond Law School
Bill Kilduff – University of Richmond Law School
Warren McGraw – Wake Forest University
Tim Manchin – West Virginia University
David Ziegler – University of Virginia
Ann Ramsey (Paralegal) – University of Richmond Law School
*Derek Swope – Washington and Lee University
*Bill Flanigan – West Virginia University
*William Henry Sanders, III – West Virginia University
*Gregory Prudich – University of Texas

*Remain in firm, Sanders, Austin, Swope and Flanigan.

THE SECRETARY OF THE NAVY

WASHINGTON

The President of the United States takes pleasure in presenting the NAVY CROSS to

FIRST LIEUTENANT WILLIAM H. SANDERS, II,
UNITED STATES MARINE CORPS RESERVE,

for service as set forth in the following

CITATION:

"For extraordinary heroism as a Reconnaissance Officer of Company D, First Battalion, Second Marines, Second
Marine Division, in action against enemy Japanese forces on
Tarawa Atoll, Gilbert Islands, 21 November 1943. When intense
fire from enemy shore emplacements inflicted heavy casualties
on our forces as they waded toward the beach, First Lieutenant
Sanders voluntarily prepared to attack the hostile positions
with the aid of a Sergeant of his company. Bringing a 75-mm.
pack howitzer into use and neutralizing the devastating fire of
the first pillbox, he courageously rushed the position despite
heavy fire from another emplacement and destroyed the pillbox
with hand grenades, moving inside immediately thereafter to
kill any remaining defenders. Under the accurate covering
fire of the Sergeant, he then crawled twenty-five yards to the
first of a group of four connecting emplacements and, completely destroying the position with TNT, unhesitatingly advanced on the second emplacement and annihilated the defenders
with hand grenades. After throwing several grenades into the
third pillbox, he entered the position and succeeded in killing
one of the Japanese before he, himself, was seriously wounded.
By his splendid initiative, First Lieutenant Sanders put out of
action three enemy .25 caliber and two 13-mm. machine guns
and one 20-mm. antiboat gun. His indomitable fighting spirit
and self-sacrificing devotion to duty were in keeping with the
highest traditions of the United States Naval Service."

For the President,

Secretary of the Navy.

239

THE SECRETARY OF THE NAVY

WASHINGTON

The President of the United States takes pleasure
in presenting the BRONZE STAR MEDAL to

FIRST LIEUTENANT WILLIAM H. SANDERS, II,
UNITED STATES MARINE CORPS RESERVE,

for service as set forth in the following

CITATION:

"For meritorious achievement while attached
to Company A, First Battalion, Second Marines,
Second Marine Division, in action against enemy
Japanese forces on Saipan and Tinian, Marianas
Islands, 8 July 1944. When his Commanding Officer
became a casualty, First Lieutenant Sanders assumed
command and continued the attack, establishing
night defense lines which successfully withstood
a hostile counterattack and effected the annihilation of three hundred and fifty Japanese troops.
His leadership, courage and devotion to duty in
the face of enemy fire were in keeping with the
highest traditions of the United States Naval
Service."

First Lieutenant Sanders is authorized to wear the
Combat "V"

For the President,

Secretary of the Navy.

240

(Excerpts from lecture to Concord College class on "Social Problems" by William Sanders, Attorney, President of Mercer-Tazewell County Council on Human Relations)
1964

THE PROBLEM

The great American experiment in democracy is now at its crucial moment. The problem of Race, North or South, is at the heart of our problem.

This great social issue is everybody's business and everybody's concern and if you don't think people are interested just take a stand and see the reaction you get. The issue of Race is close home to everybody and is of first importance to everybody, whether they admit it or try to hide from it.

America's world leadership depends on how she solves this central problem of the day. It is the key to our foreign policy. It is the key to our success and influence in the world because it is the key to our unity and national self-respect.

USEFUL PRINCIPLES

A democracy is where everybody is created equal, we simply mean that everyone must have the equal opportunity to develop his natural talents, the equal pursuit of happiness. Our great tradition is that any child born in America might become President. Certainly our Presidents prove this, even our modern Presidents, as well as Abraham Lincoln. Presently it seems that the rich man has a mighty good chance, but not long ago we had a mere haberdasher as President. At this moment I like the boldness of Attorney General Robert Kennedy when he stated that within, I believe, forty years he expected that a Negro might become President. A woman, Margaret Chase Smith, apparently recently thought that she might become President. We might have a woman President about as soon as we might have a Negro President. We recently had a member of the Roman Catholic Church as President, and this was a first. So we are still on the upgrade toward progress and democracy. But the point of my thesis is that equality of our democracy is simply the equality of opportunity.

Obviously it is a perverted idea that social equality is some kind of automatic gift to be handed to anyone on a silver platter. An equality gained in this fashion certainly would have no order and reason about it. If that were the case, all incentive would vanish, and there would be no incentive for you to spend your time and money here in college to try to equip yourself to do a

242

job.

There is one true base for status, and that is service to humanity or service to society. The person who can give the most to society is the one most highly esteemed by any society of fair-minded people.

These principles that I am driving at need badly to be said to all of us who are now struggling for correct Race relations, and they need to be said to those on both sides and to those of each Race. At the same time, it also needs badly to be said that those who sit in positions of control or what we term the POWER STRUCTURE within the various communities cannot hoard their status and their position and put a wall around it. Being better than somebody else is not an idea, but true status and position must be willing to give it away and must be ever in the process of giving it away. A person with a comfortable status does not have to worry about it and he is always trying to give it away by trying to do something for somebody less fortunate than he. It is only when our status is so uncertain and uncomfortable and so little in fact and reality that we have to try to hoard it, and we have to try to keep the other fellow down as a means of pulling ourselves up by our own bootstraps, as it were. America's influence in the world depends upon our being strong enough and sure enough to share our blessings of liberty with all mankind.

In the Race problem, these principles should be kept in mind or else the thing may devolve simply into a battle of the haves versus the have-nots or the ins versus the outs and as we often see in South America and often in Africa there is no real end to this sort of rat race.

Along the same consideration, the *status quo* of a society, a nation, or a segment of a nation can only remain quiet and peaceful so long as it recognizes and is built upon the principles I am suggesting. If the status quo is not on a basis of truth and justice, then it has no proper foundations and it should be thrown overboard just like the tea at the Boston Tea party, and we have no less authority for this than our own Thomas Jefferson who was revolutionary in the best sense.

There is no more fitting place to discuss these things, which are really moral matters, than in a college classroom. Now I am in your midst today, brought here as a practical man of the community who as a side line from the matter of earning a livelihood, is engaged in civic organizations working quietly for the benefit of civil rights. I am also in this class as a practical businessman who, for a living, deals with the disruptions of our local civil and sometimes the criminal order of society. So I am a man who, naturally, likes to have opinions, and I might even very accurately be called an opinionated sort of a person and one always on one side or the other of a controversy. I also hope that I will be called a controversial individual and when I cease to be that my productive days can be considered closed. I offer the following ideas about our local Mercer County Race relations.

THE LOCAL PICTURE

The people of West Virginia are in rebellion agianst the old power structure which really did so little for them. This cycle has not yet run. The common people of West Virginia have really been denied equal opportunity or fair opportunity and, isolated in these hills, have not realized that they have not really been getting a fair share of liberty and the pursuit of happiness.

Thus, West Virginians by and large should be sympathetic in the matter of Race relations because they are deserving of a real and true and good program for upbuilding of Appalachia, call it a poverty program or whatever you wish to call it. In the matter of Race relations in these hills, as well as in the matter of whether we are poverty stricken or not, we might not have ever known the difference if we depended solely upon our local power structures and some of our own newspapers are news media.

RACE RELATIONS MESSAGE
AT NEW CENTURY METHODIST CHURCH,
PRINCETON, WEST VIRGINIA
FEBRUARY, 1964

BY

WILLIAM SANDERS, PRESIDENT
MERCER-TAZEWELL COUNTY COUNCIL
ON HUMAN RELATIONS

Liberty in Christ

Luke 4:17, 18 and 19.

"And there was delivered unto Him the Book of the Prophet Isaiah. And when he had opened the book he found the place where it was written.

"The Spirit of the Lord is upon me, because he hath anointed me to preach the Gospel to the poor; he hath sent me to heal the brokenhearted, to preach deliverance to the captives, and recovering of sight to the blind, to set at liberty them that are bruised,

"To preach the acceptable year of the Lord.

And he closed the book, and he gave it again to the minister, and sat down, And the eyes of all them that were in the synagogue were fastened on him."

Jesus Christ was baptized by John the Baptist and straightway went into the wilderness a figurative forty days to get his bearings before launching forth on his short three years concentrated ministry on this earth and he had just been tempted in the wilderness to seek earthly power and his first act upon emerging from the wilderness was to go to church and make the pronouncement I have just read which are his own words selected from the Book of Isaiah.

Christ came into the world for the purpose of setting men free. In all reality he was put to death because he did not for a moment cease nor desist from setting men free and this disturbed the status quo and irritated those in Church and State who comprised the "power structure." He was revolutionary and everything he did in his short ministry was done toward the equality of mankind, for the liberty of those suffering any form of oppression. And he personally and single-handedly extended the covenant of God to each and every man on an equal basis – he was utterly no respecter of persons and he determined at the very outset that he would not seek out the rich nor the influential to accomplish his mission even if a few of those did seek out him.

The New Testament and Christianity stand for equality and Brotherhood under Fatherhood – There is no circumcision, no bond nor free, male nor female, black nor white – the Christian Church is here to break down and not to build up all the walls of separation. In our town, our churches have not yet been big enough to open their doors, their arms and their hearts to class and race, and in so doing they are serving only to give false status to a prestige-mad, small-minded citizenry, and there is something vitally lacking in their worship – the Holy Spirit is on the outside and we will not "get moving again" until the Holy Spirit is invited to come in and dwell on the inside of an inclusive fellowship.

The really great causes of the world are primarily the Church's causes and these are simply Humanity and Unity. And still the church people have their minds centered on the little things which build pride and divide people.

It is the Church which should be at the forefront of revolution and if it is not there, then change lacks direction and true purpose. This applies to freedom marches and freedom movements among the Negroes both here and the world around.

Even those who were nearest to Christ did not understand what He was truly about. Only His enemies understood because those who held the evil power were directly affected – He hit them where it hurt. But people generally could only catch the vision of His purpose after He died and the Holy Spirit visited among them and the Holy Spirit dictated to them the New Testament from God for ALL men.

Mankind's advance in freedom came to a new threshold with Christ and with Christ it advances still.

Not just we Gentiles, but particular classes of people very directly owe their freedom to Jesus Christ, and one of these is woman. Women should know this fact, that they were set free of the shackles of slavery and made more than mere chattel, through Jesus Christ, and women thus are in what we term these days a minority group and they thus are enabled to be more sympathetic to the cause of Negro freedom than are men generally. To depart a bit, President Kennedy was of a minority group, the Boston Irish, and thus he could well know the aspirations and sufferings of the Negro. And this brings me to discuss the important meaning of the term in the Scripture I have read to you, "to set at liberty those who are bruised." Bruised is like "second-class citizenship," that is, second-class citizenship bruises and scars and warps and embitters a personality. Anyone who has known second-class citizenship – like Kennedy from snob Boston – knows what it can do to the spirit of man. This is the kind of thing that the fierce writer, James Baldwin, writes about.

Second-class citizenship bruising can cause ill mental health among Negroes, unless they are in the Church and they know the presence of Christ. They may become bruised and stunted in their growth, perhaps even to the point that thay are caused to just spend their lives standing around the wasting their time in total nothingness, neither helping themselves nor doing any good for anyone else. Or maybe they just become sullen and sour on the world.

It is the bruising which is so brutal and so bad and which destroys constructive citizenship,a nd thoughtul people are trying to do something about it. Thus, the great Judges of the United States Supreme Court pronounced that separate schooling is inherently unequal schooling – it is second-class schooling and it has a great tendency to leave that kind of a mark on the student and penalize his life accordingly.

Getting back to the case of women, I was just this past week comparing with one of your members last Sunday's International Sunday School lesson on the meeting of Christ with the Samaritan woman at the well when she was set free. The emancipation of woman is a case in point also for the fact that the process is not to be completed in a flash and it is still going on sluggishly and we still hear that women should "stay in their places." However, somehow, we can't keep them in their places because Christ is still saying to women to advance in knowledge, wisdom and truth, and today, in America especially, and in the world following suit, women very often make the difference in honest politics, government, jury service, et cetera.

Why is it that poor people are generally more religious than others, and I believe they are? Because Christ is truly at work with them and they are not deluded with the thought that they are earning salvation.

And why are Negroes religious? Why are there so many Negro churches, here and in any town? Why do the freedom marches most always start and go forth from Negro churches – because Christ sets them in motion. Nothing is more fitting than this.

Christ is the most revolutionary figure the world has ever known but He did not organize armies nor compose organizations nor seek out the influential people although His followers continually urged this upon Him. Rather, He set the pattern of taking upon himself the problems of the oppressed and he singly stood in direct opposition to every form of tyranny over the spirit of man, both in the Church and out of the Church. He told His disciples to do likewise, individually and on the same pattern He set, and that they did after His leaving them.

It was this courage which President Kennedy called the supreme virtue. And Christ set the pattern for all other men of concern and good will – the pattern of the suffering servent which was assumed by Abraham Lincoln as largely as any man in the modern age when Abraham Lincoln chose to bear the crosses of the little and the oppressed who had no one to speak for them. Abraham Lincoln also carried with him a dread sense of destiny and personal doom and yet he could not have done otherwise than speak for mankind's freedom where the battle of freedom was taking place here in America.

The same seems in this short view of history to be also true of President Kennedy in that he did what he had to do regardless of popularity and despite the fact that he was a man like Lincoln who loved people and loved to be loved by people. Each of these ment knew – could not help but know that they were surely and steadily lighting the fires of resentment which would destroy them. Such men gave themselves over to history's God, Who first loved them at their mother's knee and whose love they compelled to return. Christ set this pattern, this price for freedom, of enough men and women returning the love of God and presenting their bodies a living sacrifice as their reasonable service, and this is the "eternal vigilance" which is the "price of liberty." And such men and women of vigilance are never separated from the love of Christ which strengthens them.

To conclude, by virtue of studying the Holy Scriptures in the light of the issues of today, I am convinced that the New Testament and that the Christ of the New Age of history unerringly purposes that freedom is for every man – that salvation is free. If my life had not been touched by a study of the Scriptures, I am sure that I would have felt that every advantage that is mine is deserved and that others without such advantages simply don't deserve them.

And I look upon our world with the brighter hope – that the American Negro is a bright and saving force among men, and particularly in America. The Negro brings to America a great new spirit. His soul is rising and he is on the move toward greater service and accomplishment and this fact is keeping America from social stagnation and will let America see and do its higher duty in the world.

America is singularly blessed in having her Negroes and God moves in mysterious ways in implanting you here. Our partnership in Christianitya nd Democracy is our opportunity to unlock the solution of war and peace in the world adn we are surely achieving something unique in America in the form of racial brotherhood. The Negro has advanced greatly in America and is only now beginning to really realize his worth as a child of God. Way back at the beginning of Christ's ministry He said that it should be so, and with Christ's help it will be so.

Sunday morning sermon at New Century Methodist Church (Black) in Princeton, West Virginia in February 1964, by William Sanders, President of Mercer-Tazewell County Council on Human Relations is here copied again from the original.

Princeton Times

A Daily Newspaper Devoted Exclusively to the Progress of
This Community
Princeton, West Virginia, Tuesday, February 12, 1963
Guest Editorial . . .

American Civil Rights
By William Sanders

The American Revolution was founded on equal rights and it was declared man was created equal and had the unalienable right to life, liberty and the pursuit of happiness.

However, Abraham Lincoln pointed to the deterioration of this great principle of revolution prior to the Civil War in his famous Peoria reply to Douglas, saying:

"Little by little, but steadily as man's march to the grave, we have been giving up the old for the new faith. Near eighty years ago we began by declaring that all men are created equal; but now from that beginning we have run down to the other declaration that for some men to enslave others is a 'sacred right of self-government.' These principles cannot stand together. They are as opposite as God and mammon; whoever holds to the one must despise the other."

Again in that speech Lincoln spoke of slavery as "fatally devouring the noblest political system the world every saw."

And so the Civil War was fought for the same ideal of equal rights and significantly this war was fought by white man against white man to win rights of negroes. And yet it is still largely argued that this was not the real purpose of that complicated Civil War. But the proposition will remain that the Nation could no longer endure half slave and half free.

Following the Civil War our Nation for 100 years relapsed into a concept of "separate but equal" rights for the races. In this fashion a great multitude of Americans, in the same frame of mind and weak heart of those who refuse to recognize why the Civil War was fought, will tell you that there is no race problem in America – that the negro is satisfied with his lot and that things should be allowed to take their "natural course."

However, the Supreme Court has now historically pro-

251

nounced that "separate is inherently unequal" and thus has redeclared that fundamental principle which is the very foundation stone of our Nationhood – equality.

And in the land today, American white and American negro are joining hands in this great heritage. Much new progress is being made to the end that there will be no chip on the shoulder of either white or colored and each will become equal members of the same community.

We should ask ourselves what progress have we made to end discrimination of the races in our town – in church (where it should begin) – in school – in shop – in stores, etc. And does a bright and promising young negro have to leave this community to find employment equal to his ability or should we rather expect him to remain around to do our odd jobs?

The Course

From far up in the night's sky a brilliant moon looks down through flying clouds, sending a silver shaft along the ship's wake. As far as the eye can observe stretches the glimmering sheen on the surface of the sea.

There lies the world on its glamorous avenue, first, slashing, clashing, bubbling, boiling. Then, in the distance, gradually settling into an even, gently rippling current of harmony, all waves absorbed and all parts subdued by the larger strength and cohesion of the whole. Until, in the farthest reaches of the brightness the course seems to flow into one large stilled calm lake of living together, each part and particle identically one and rapturously serene.

BOOKS BY WILLIAM SANDERS

1. *Legacy of Homes and Families / Princeton-Athens Area / West Virginia*
   A history of the towns through its prominent early families and the homes they built
   1985, 132 pages, indexed, with maps, photos and illustrations
      Walsworth Publishing, Marceline, MO.

2. *Lilly on the Bluestone* (Third Edition Enlarged)
   The story of the first two generations of the Lilly-Meador(ows) family settlement on the Bluestone.
   1989, 100 pages, indexed with illustrations, photos and cemetery map. Revised 1997.
      McClain Printing Company, Parsons, West Virginia
      (Third Printing in Progress)

3. *A New River Heritage, Volume I*
   Exploration and first settlements along the River from George Pearis' settlement at Pearisburg to Island Creek, accounts of Indians, families, slaves, marriages and cemeteries.
   1992, 298 pages, with index of family cemeteries, maps, photos and illustrations.
      McClain Printing Company, Parsons, West Virginia

4. *A New River Heritage, Volume II*
   The story of River settlement continued from Island Creek and Lick Creek and Crumps bottom through the Pipestem area, including settlements such as Lilly on the Bluestone and Farley, early families and cemeteries
   1992, 400 pages, with index of family cemeteries, maps, photos and illustrations.
      McClain Printing Company, Parsons, West Virginia

5. *A New River Heritage, Volume III*
   Details settlement along the River at Hinton, Madam's Creek and Jumping Branch, including Pack's Ferry and the creation of Summers County, lists all the cemeteries of the first 200 families which were moved when the Bluestone Dam was constructed,

CONTAINS NAME INDEX FOR THE FIRST THREE VOL-UMES.
1994, 332 pages, with index of cemeteries, maps, photos and illustrations
McClain Printing Company, Parsons, West Virginia

6. *A New River Heritage, Volume IV*
Flat Top, Camp Creek and Bluestone settlements off the New River, includes selected stories of the late Barty Wyatt and an account of the early life of US Senator Robert C. Byrd, also Bailey–Davidson, Bluestone headwater settlement
1994, 429 pages, with name index, maps, photos and illustrations
McClain Printing Company, Parsons, West Virginia

7. *Early Princeton and the Episcopal Church*
Early Princeton and the political battles with Athens and Bluefield over the seat of Mercer County Courthouse, and the origin of first churches (being revised.)
1993, 87 pages, indexed, with maps, photos and reproduced original records
McClain Printing Company, Parsons, West Virginia

8. *On the Skirmish Line*
Autobiography, from 1917 to present, early childhood in Princeton, college years, in the Marine Corps fighting the Japanese in the South Pacific, on the General Staff of the occupation government in Berlin, return to West Virginia, early law practice and family life, civil rights, and environmental concerns; and,
Accounts of interesting cases and reflections upon the practice of law based upon a life in court litigating cases both criminal and civil, throughout Southern West Virginia, – philosophical, warm and insightful.
1997, 300 pages, with maps, photos and illustrations
McClain Printing Company, Parsons, West Virginia

Copies of all volumes are available from the author, write
or call:
William Sanders
320 Courthouse Road
Princeton, West Virginia 24740
Telephone: (304) 425-8125 (office) – (304) 425-9436 (home)
Fax: (304) 425-4155